Rambles
in
North Wales

Roger Redfern

Published by Sigma Leisure – an imprint of
Sigma Press, 1 South Oak Lane, Wilmslow, Cheshire SK9 6AR, England.

British Library Cataloguing in Publication Data
A CIP record for this book is available from the British Library.

ISBN: 1-85058-350-1

Typesetting and Design by: Sigma Press, Wilmslow, Cheshire.

Maps by: Morag Perrott

Text photographs: Roger Redfern

Cover photograph: Nant Peris from Crib-y-Ddysgl (Roger Redfern)

Printed by: Interprint Ltd, Malta

General Disclaimer

Foreword

I was brought up and now live among the mountains of North Wales about which Mr Redfern writes, and so I am most vulnerable to his statement that North Wales is his "mountain home": by saying this, he at once has me on his side.

Too many of us forget that the mountain areas of Wales, and even of the Snowdonia National Park, are not confined to the relatively small and compact group of Snowdon itself, distinctive as that group is. Even for those living in Liverpool, Chester, and Shrewsbury, "I'm going to Wales this week-end" has come to mean "I'm going to Snowdon, or to within a ten-mile radius of it." I myself must plead guilty to this narrow view, for I recently committed the solecism of saying to a Cardiff man in Cardiff, when I was setting out for my home at Capel Curig on a day of bright sunshine, "Don't you wish you were coming with me to Wales?" It is therefore welcome to find Mr Redfern drawing attention to Lleyn, to Cadair Idris, to Arenig, and to the Aran.

In Wales Mr Redfern has ranged far beyond the bounds of "Eryri" and in this volume his breadth of taste is reflected, to the great benefit and pleasure of the reader. The walker who follows in Mr Redfern's footsteps will in particular reap a rich harvest. He must be a hardy walker and often must know something of rough mountain going for Mr Redfern's paths are not smooth, and very often the roughest ones are those on which most easily to get the feel of Welsh mountain land.

Mr Redfern has much to say about the wild, empty country between Bala, Trawsfynydd and Dolgellau, by a happy chance the scene of my own first solitary journey as a boy with a tent, a journey which left me with lasting romantic memories of secret valleys, wide vistas bound by mysterious ranges and brief encounters with small, bad-tempered, black Welsh bulls. When Mr Redfern takes us to out-of-the-way places his knowledge of history and local affairs helps the reader to enjoy the country in ways which are impossible to the uninitiated.

Mr Redfern likes the wild spots and I hope that many will be led by this book to visit places off the beaten track, and led also to explore in detail by reading elsewhere the local history and folklore to which Mr Redfern has of necessity within the scope of this book only been able to give pointers. I hope too that when the reader visits some of Mr Redfern's wild places he will do so equipped in mind and body to enjoy himself, as much as ever when the mists hide every landmark and the wild Welsh rain drives across the scene, changing a pleasant country ramble into the cold, damp, nervous encounter with the unknown that is an enchanting and necessary part of getting to know and love the Welsh mountains.

CHARLES EVANS

Contents

Location map

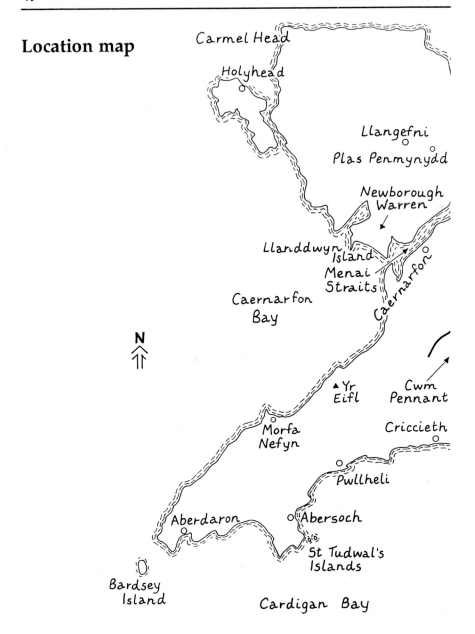

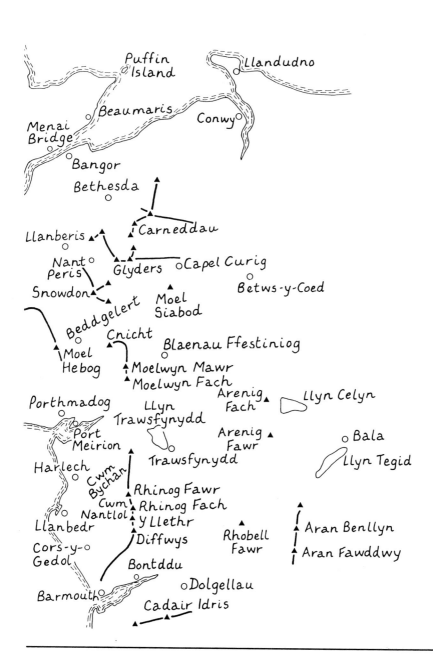

Introduction

The sea played a more important role in transport in former ages than did the land, especially the difficult land of upland Britain, the region of older rocks which is thought of in general terms as Highland Britain.

MacKinder considered that "the land unites, the seas divide" but in upland regions it is possible to state categorically (over eighty years after his death) that "the land divides, the seas unite". Nowhere is this influence better seen than in the western extremities of Wales. Here we must confine ourselves to North Wales but this district is but part of a larger region centred upon the Irish Sea.

The highest mountains were navigating points to the Ancients, markers at the frontiers of an oceanic region. Consider the highest points of the Wicklow Mountains, the Mountains of Mourne, the hills of Galloway, Snaefell in the Isle of Man, the heights of Cumbria and the mountains of Snowdonia -all were visible in clear weather from the next and were used as navigating points when Nature allowed it.

Professor E. G. Bowen has clearly pointed out that the peninsulas and currents and whirlpools and seas are more important than the mountains, the valleys and the bogs when considering the archaeology of the west, and this inevitably includes North Wales. MacKinder's regional province of the South-west Approaches is a cultural province; the cult of St David spread throughout South Wales, Cornwall and Brittany just as the cult of St. Brendan spread throughout north-western Ireland and the Hebrides.

There are, then, three provinces in Britain-not just the two MacKinder referred to as Highland and Lowland (the areas of old and new rocks respectively)-and these three are Highland, Lowland and Atlantic Britain. The latter is, really, the narrow margin of low land below six hundred feet separating Highland Britain from the western sea. In places it does not exist, as where high cliffs fall straight from the mountain-tops.

In this book I have ranged far to the north and south of the highest peaks of Snowdonia, which is truly the core of the region. My region of "North Wales" extends from Cadair Idris in the south to Anglesey's north coast, a distance of sixty miles; from the high ridge of the Arans in the east to the wild, western tip of the Lleyn peninsula and Bardsey Island, a distance of fifty miles.

I have of necessity had to confine myself to this region; roughly, but not entirely, to the area enclosed within the borders of the Snowdonia National Park. To me this area is an entity with a completeness which would have been spoilt by including some of the uplands of mid-Wales to the south and the Denbigh Moors to the east.

This book, then, ranges over an exquisite part of our islands which contains part of two of the regions referred to earlier; there is the central heart of true Highland and the narrow margin of Atlantic Britain which acts as a bountiful necklace, precious jewels encircling a wondrous body of high hills and lakes and vapours.

To each his own reasons for love of the earth's high places. For me the mountains of Snowdonia are "home" in a mountain sense. I came to them as a baby and have never stopped returning. I grew with them, the atmosphere of Welsh mountains is part of me and will remain so.

The familiar, old, grey rock; the staghorn moss in wet and secret arbors below the crests; the coming and going of a thousand lights and cloud-forms; the forgotten habitations of men and beasts in lonely valleys; these are the things of North Wales. The language which echoes in the hill shapes and in the valleys and coves, spoken softly or strong, sung by one or one hundred, the Welsh voice is music, the language a dream of loveliness befitting a lovely land. These things and the closeness of the sea, just out of sight beyond a range of high hills, are the charms of North Wales. I can do little to describe them adequately to the stranger. My hope is that he may discover some of the happiness that I have found here, a happiness derived from a combination of many things, and perhaps it is that enigma called "atmosphere" which casts the strongest spell of all.

Parc Cenedlaethol Eryri, (the Snowdonia National Park) was established in 1951 and has an area of 845 square miles and is the second largest National Park in Britain, being slightly less in area than the Lake District National Park. This book extends beyond the limits of this park, notably in the chapters devoted to the Lleyn peninsula and Anglesey.

Sixty square miles of the Lleyn peninsula have been designated as an Area of Outstanding Natural Beauty. This means that the area is in the care of the local planning authority and its landscape beauty can be maintained and improved.

There are five notable nature reserves in the area covered by this book. One is the 1,565 acres of Newborough Warren-Yns Llanddwyn in south-western Anglesey; another is lovely Cwm Idwal beneath the northern flank of Glyder Fawr; the third occupies 969 acres of Cadair Idris at the southern border of the National Park; the fourth nature reserve is 991 acres of those loneliest of far hills, the Rhinogs, and the fifth is the reserve established on the cliffs of Allt-wen, the Tremadoc cliffs. Access is unlimited to these reserves, except in the Newborough Warren-Ynys Llanddwyn reserve, where permits are required if one wishes to wander off rights of way. The reserves are administered by The Countryside Council for Wales.

Which are the best centres for exploring North Wales on foot? I recommend the following:

BALA: A pleasant inland market town with an unusually wide main street and not far from the eastern end of Llyn Tegid (Bala Lake). A good centre from which to explore the Arans and the Arenigs.

DOLGELLAU: The main town of Merionethshire, hidden by high hills and not far from the head of the Mawddach valley. A fine place from which to explore Cadair Idris and the hills of the southern Harlech Dome.

BARMOUTH: Out of the holiday season a quiet Cardigan Bay-side resort and well placed from which to explore Cadair Idris, the Mawddach estuary and the southern Harlech Dome.

HARLECH: An ancient market town on Cardigan Bay and well placed for explorations of the central and northern hills of the Harlech Dome.

FFESTINIOG: A hill-side settlement above the beautiful Vale of Ffestiniog and possibly the best centre for rambles into the lonely hill country of Migneint to the east, the rarely-trodden hills between Bala and Trawsfynydd, and the slaty mountains encircling Blaenau-Ffestiniog.

BEDDGELERT: Beautifully sited, this notable holiday centre is excellent for the Moel Hebog group, the southern flanks of the Snowdon massif and the Cnicht-Moelwyn complex. One of the most attractively-sited villages in the whole of Wales but best nowadays out of the holiday season.

CAPEL CURIG: Well placed for the Carneddau, the Glyder group and the Snowdon massif. This upland village on the London-Holyhead road is an important place at the time of the annual sales of Welsh Mountain Sheep.

NANT PERIS: A lovely, ancient village, mountain-girt, and ideal for explorations of the Snowdon, Glyder and Elidir massifs. Again, at its best when the "tourist" has not arrived or has gone home.

CRICCIETH: A seaside town on Cardigan Bay's northern shore well situated for rambles on Moel Hebog and not far from many of the hills of the Lleyn peninsula.

MENAI BRIDGE; A bustling settlement on Anglesey's south coast. A good centre from which to explore that island's varied charms.

Times have changed since the end of the eighteenth century when the only inns in Snowdonia were two cottages at Beddgelert. Besides the above centres there are dozens of smaller villages, often less easy to reach but offering many advantages and delights. Part of the charm of rambling in North Wales will be gained by finding them, so that a return may be made for further exploration of another corner yet untrodden.

Most of the small villages can offer some accommodation, and many remote farms will put up the rambler. If food and shelter cannot be found there is always the prospect of camping in some high valley, some cloudy cwm or quiet lake-side under trees.

As one wanders through this mountain area the two farm animals that are most often noticed are the Welsh Black cattle and Welsh Mountain sheep.

The Welsh Black is one of the most ancient of cattle breeds, strongly resembling the cattle which roamed our island before the Roman invasion. The present day animal is the result of a merger of the North Wales or Anglesey breed with Castle Martin, Pembroke or South Wales breed. It can produce milk of high quality in conditions which would almost kill many less hardy breeds. The North Wales breed was really a beef animal and large numbers of these cattle were, and still are, fattened on Midland pastures (known there as Welsh Runts).

The Welsh Mountain sheep is typical of breeds which inhabit Britain's highest land-small, sure-footed and very hardy. The horns of the ram of this pale-faced Welsh Mountain breed are large and finely curved. Though the wool is soft and fine it is as a meat producer that the breed is best known-Welsh mutton is world famous.

The animals of these two breeds have changed only little since the days of the notable early travellers, those enlightened men like George Borrow, John Ruskin, Charles Kingsley and Charles Edward Mathews. Pioneers who found beauty and hidden glory and romance in the high hills. Like them let us return to the hills again and again, return and escape to the lovely hills of North Wales.

Maps and Map References

Four maps are needed to follow all the walks in this book. They are the Ordnance Survey "Landranger" series (1:50,000 scale) numbered 114 (Anglesey), 115 (Snowdon and Surrounding Area), 123 (Pwllheli) and 124 (Dolgellau and Surrounding Area).

For greater detail and interest three maps in the Ordnance Survey "Outdoor Leisure" series (1:25,000 scale) are recommended. They are numbered 17 (Snowdonia – Snowdon and Conwy Valley areas), 18 (Snowdonia – Harlech and Bala areas) and 23 (Snowdonia – Cadair Idris and Bala areas).

The map references are given so that a check may be kept on one's route if this is desired and if doubts arise from the descriptions in the text. These map references only apply, of course, to the map mentioned in the introductory notes to each walk.

Reading a Map Reference

Ordnance Survey maps are divided into one-kilometre squares formed by imaginary lines which are numbered around the map margins. These lines are identical on the 1:50,000 and 1:25,000 scale maps.

If one is finding map reference 687/694 on the 1:50,000 Ordnance Survey map 115 (Snowdon and Surrounding Area):

(i) Look along the northern margin of the map for number 68 and then divide the area between 68 and 69 into ten imaginary sections, each one-tenth of a kilometre apart. Continue eastwards beyond 68 for seven-tenths of the distance to 69.

(ii) Look up the eastern margin of the map for number 69 and then divide the area between 69 and 70 into ten imaginary sections, each again one-tenth of a kilometre apart. Continue northwards beyond 69 for four-tenths of the distance to 70.

(iii) Now we have two points on the margins of the map – 68-7 on the northern margin and 69-4 on the eastern margin. Where imaginary lines are drawn through these points parallel to the printed lines the point at which they intersect is the map reference referred to – in this case the summit of Llwydmor in the northern Carneddau.

Mention must here be made of the fact that some of these walks seem very short. For instance, the second ramble on Cadair Idris is only five miles in length. One must remember that in mountain country a comparatively short distance on the map takes far longer in practice due to the effects of steep and rugged ground. Allowance should be made for this when planning these walks.

Chapter 1

SLATE FROM THE HILLS

Towards the end of the Ordovician geological era earth movements affected and altered the Cambrian shales of parts of what is now North Wales. A stable north-western block of pre-Cambrian rock running parallel with the present site of the Menai Straits (today known as the Padarn Ridge) acted as an immovable object against which the earth movements had little effect. The resulting pressure, on a scale inconceivable to man, so affected the structure of the shales lying to the south of this Padarn Ridge that they turned into what we call slate.

Because the constituent particles all lie in the same direction slate can be split into strong and durable parallel-sided sheets, a property known as "hollt" to the Welsh and better known as "cleavage".

Because the pressure came from the south-east the great slate quarries of North Wales lie in the strip of country immediately to the south of the Padarn Ridge – in the Nantlle, Llanberis and Bethesda districts. Another important area for slate quarrying was further to the south, centred upon the drab town of Blaenau Ffestiniog.

> *Cambrian shales have altered state*
> *Pressed by a mountain storm*
> *Into even harder slate.*
> *Dinorwic makes the roofs at a rate*
> *To keep the Welsh rain out*
> *Caused by those mountains of slate.*

I agree with the assertion that slate quarrying is, in a sense, the most "Welsh" of all Welsh industries. Although it has been obtained since Roman times the quarrying of slate did not become the major industry of Caernarvonshire until the improvements to roads. A century and a half ago slates were dragged on horse-drawn sledges to the nearest track, where carts took them away – usually to Felin Heli (later re-named Port Dinorwig) on the Menai Straits.

The construction of a tram-road between Dinorwig Quarry, above Llanberis, and Port Dinorwig in 1824-5 led to a rapid development of that gigantic quarry, so that by 1926 eight hundred men were producing 20,000 tons of slate a year. This is a very great amount, especially when one realises that to produce one ton of slate involves the quarrying of between twelve and twenty tons of useless rock! Little surprise, then, at the great amount of Elidir Fawr's south-western ridge and flanks that has been broken away.

By the 1860s Dinorwig Quarry was producing 100,000 tons of slate annually, while the Penrhyn Quarry (on the far side of the mountain near Bethesda) was producing even more, and employed 2,500 men in 1892. The smaller quarries at Nantlle and Gwyrfai nearly trebled production during the middle years of the last century – from 25,300 tons in 1852 to 73,900 tons by 1882. This development and the consequent full employment in this area of relatively little industrial activity can be said to have resulted in a demand for slates on two accounts; the great spate of building throughout Britain due to an increase of 10,000 miles of railways between 1848 and 1877 on the one hand, and the phenomenal growth in the export of slate, especially to Germany.

During the present century the industry has contracted considerably, largely a result of the decline in domestic consumption of roofing slates which went with the increasing use of other roofing materials. It is interesting to note here that in 1900 four out of five new houses were roofed with slates, but by 1938 only one new house was roofed with slates to every four roofed with clay or concrete tiles. As 97 per cent of Snowdonia's slate production was roofing slates it is easy to see the reason for the industry's decline.

By 1946 there were only 2,955 men employed in slate quarrying in Snowdonia and now the industry is virtually dead. The scars are weathering on the hills into obscurity. One turns a shoulder of the hill and sees there, above Nant Peris and Rhyd-ddu and in a hundred odd corners, the ruins of quarries slowly reverting to the wild.

The great quarries in the flanks of the Moelwyns above Blaenau Ffestiniog are closed down. Here, by the way, folding of the slate stratum millions of years ago made it necessary to dig tunnels and shafts to obtain the best slates. In the great pass between Cnicht and Moelwyn Mawr one comes across a whole, grey world of empty slate buildings, rows of cottages in fact, and mountains of half-worked slates. This derelict area is indeed intriguing and one can spend hours exploring man's endeavours hereabouts. When the clouds are low and rain crosses the pass in sheets it is a world of sadness and not a lot of imagination is required to see men at work among the wet and purple slates. Yes, in my mind Welsh slates are "normal" when they glisten in the rain, reflecting low, flying clouds riding the breasts of the slaty hills.

Slate fence, Nant Peris, Gwynedd

Chapter 2

KING ARTHUR IN SNOWDONIA

The name Arthur certainly looks Welsh, at least Celtic in spelling and in sound. Whether this man really existed is still a matter for conjecture and the imagination. Recent research in southern England tends to suggest that there was an Arthur, though not the medieval armour-clad character who has featured for so long in the traditional stories of the Round Table, the Holy Grail and Excalibur, a romantic figure who really originated at the pen of Geoffrey of Monmouth, the clerk born at the very beginning of the twelfth century.

It was the fifteenth-century Warwickshire knight St Thomas Malory who set the Arthurian legend in its well-known and well-loved setting of Medieval England, of armour-clad knights and dark woods beneath towering castle walls. Later tellers of the tale followed this romantic version, tellers which included Tennyson and William Morris.

Gawaine was one of the Knights of the Round Table and his name is perpetuated elsewhere in the medieval writings centred upon the north-west Midlands – "Sir Gawaine and the Green Knight" is a notable and mysterious story set on the borders of Staffordshire and Derbyshire and one place referred to in the story has, by recent research, been identified as Lud's Church, a gritstone ravine above the Dane Valley. Clearly this character of Arthuriana has spilt over into other literature. Has not the whole story become diffused and utilised by the writer of fiction to such an extent that what is fact and what imaginings is no longer clear to us because of the sheer passage of time, and of fancy?

It is probably true to state that Arthur was a British leader who lived soon after the Romans left these islands in A.D. 411. He it would be that drew together the British tribes to repel the invasions of the Saxons from the south and east. It is not unreasonable, then, to expect his strongholds to be in the west, and that is where most places of association with Arthur are found. It is quite probable that the main court or headquarters of his native army was in south-west England, in Somerset. Excavations undertaken revealed a whole court at South Cadbury, near Glastonbury. Is this Camelot? And is Glastonbury Tor the place called Avalon, where Arthur is supposedly buried?

The places in North Wales, especially in Snowdonia, associated with Arthur are legion. Reference to maps will soon show the whereabouts of many of these sites; suggesting that here the ancient British fighters for freedom were driven by the advancing Saxons, into a mountain and coastal fastness far from their lowland headquarters. Maybe these are the last places of our islands that the Celtic defender-king and his men saw before being over-run and defeated.

In the lovely wooded mid-reaches of Nant Gwynant a little below Llyn Dinas stand the wondrous remains of a stone fort upon a low hill-top called Dinas Emrys. Only the stone foundations now remain, mossy beneath the oak and ash woods. This is traditionally the ancient place which Vortigern, betraying king of the British who allowed his land to fall to the invading Saxons under Hengist and Horsa, had erected for the apparent defence of his people. Following the instructions of his wise men Vortigern had a boy "without a mortal father" brought here to be sacrificed, his spilt blood causing the evil spirits to go, spirits which had thrice thrown down the fortress during its construction. The boy brought was Ambrosius Merlinus, the marvellous wonder boy of the fifth century. His wisdom before King Vortigern saved his life and, to quote Dr. Ernest A. Baker, this boy became "celebrated in legend and literature as the great soothsayer and wonder-worker, Merlin".

The Merlin story, centred at Dinas Emrys, was set down fully in a literary form by Nennius in the "Historia Britonum", a work written in the seventh and eighth centuries.

Legend must play a large part, perhaps fortunately, in the story of Arthurian characters and happenings in North Wales. From the medieval *Red Book of Hergest* the notable Welsh tales in the book called *Mabinogion* contain many fine tales of the noble warrior and his followers; tales excellently translated by Lady Charlotte Guest. Who can contradict out of hand that Arthur rested by and drank from the chalybeate well a mile to the south-east of Llanddeiniolen, a spring for centuries called Ffynnon Cegin Arthur? Did not the noble Celt stand upon the round summit of Moelfre, between the Rhinogs and Cardigan Bay, even if he did not hurl his Quoit from that place to the boggy levels below?

Long ago a shepherd related how he happened upon a cave high up on Craig Cwrwgl (the Pillar of Elidir). The cave was found to contain King Arthur's treasure.

The tale is recounted by J. M. Archer Thomson in his book *Climbing in the Ogwen District*, published in 1910. Great confusion resulted from the shepherd's entry into the cave and he turned to flee but as he looked out and down to the waters of Llyn Marchlyn Mawr he "beheld thereon a coracle in which sat three women of more than mortal beauty, but the dread aspect of the rower would have filled the stoutest heart with terror". The dreadful rower may be associated with King Arthur's treasure.

At the head of Cwm-y-Llan lies the small amphitheatre of Cwm Tregalan, where there once stood the traditional city of Tregalan. King Arthur supposedly defeated his enemies – whether invading Saxons or treacherous Celts – and drove them up to the watershed, to the pass which sweeps down between Lliwedd and Y Wyddfa and is called Bwlch-y-Saethau, the Pass of the Arrows. The late E. W. Steeple records that "when he reached the top of the pass the enemy let fly a shower of arrows, and Arthur was fatally wounded". There stood (and maybe still stands) upon the wide and windswept col a very ancient cairn – not the pile of stones marking the turn of the Watkin Path below Lliwedd's last upthrust – known from ancient times as Carnedd Arthur. After their leader's death his knights went across the precipitous face of Lliwedd to a cave called Ogof Llanciau Eryri. The cave "immediately closed, and the young men sleep, resting on their shields, awaiting the second coming of the King". It is recorded that a shepherd ventured near this cave long ago and glimpsed the glint of shining armour from within, he went in, hit his head of a hanging bell and woke the sleeping warriors and returned to the valley a changed man.

Llyn Llydaw lies far below Bwlch-y-Saethau and Lliwedd's north-facing cliffs. It is thought that this lake's name is a proper one, though it is also the Welsh for Armorica, another title for Brittany, where there are traces and connections with the Arthurian legend. When the lake was partly drained during the nineteenth century the remains of an ancient vessel, a type of canoe, were found. The imagination catches hold of the Arthurian barge of legend, though it seems that the canoe is of a type always associated with lake dwellings in ancient times.

The great scholar Sir John Rhys has given lustre to the tales of Arthur and the possibility of his presence hereabouts in the far-off long-ago. "With the eyes of Malory we seem to watch Bedivere making, with Excalibur in his hands, his three reluctant journeys to the lake ere he yielded it to the arm emerging from the deep."

Was the mortally wounded king carried down from Bwlch-y-Saethau to the dark, still shore of Llydaw to be carried off by "a lytyl barge with many fayre ladyes in hit", accompanied by mourning and loud lamentation? Sir John Rhys suggests, though, (in his *Celtic Folklore*, published in 1901) that the other tale of Llyn Marchlyn Mawr and the coracle containing the "three wondrously fair women" may be part of the same whole; a leader-king taken away over the steely, lapping lake-waters beneath grey-black, cloud-wrapped cliffs and, glinting in the first dawn-light creeping over Moel Siabod, Excalibur held straight and high by a bold-lined arm, washed by the wake of the passed vessel carrying off the passing Arthur into the intensifying light of another day, another age.

Chapter 3

AT THE HEAD OF THE PASS

The deep and rocky valley drained by the Afon Nant Peris divides dramatically the massifs of Snowdon and the Glyders. A place long avoided by route-makers, it was only used as a shepherd's track, a way for driving sheep down towards the northern coastal plain or southwards towards markets in Merionethshire.

Even the Romans ignored it, creating a road between Tomen-y-Mûr (near present-day Trawsfynydd) and Segontium (Caernarfon) by way of Beddgelert and Llyn Cwellyn. From Tomen-y-Mûr another road crossed the moors to the Conwy Valley and Conovium (near Tal-y-Cafn) and another route crossed a shoulder of the northern Carneddau, along the northern coastal plain to Segontium.

Thomas Telford improved and re-routed much of the track through the Ogwen Valley and so down the Nant Ffrancon, creating the modern Holyhead Road. The wild pass of Llanberis remained wild.

There were a few isolated farmsteads at the head of Nant Cynnyd above Nant Gwynant and one or two farms stood in the deep shadows of Llanberis Pass, placed like Ynys Ettws and Blaen-y-nant, but few travellers crossed the wild Pen-y-Pass ("the head of the pass") at 1,169 feet above sea level. Up to the middle of the last century there was nothing but two heaps of stones at Pen-y-Pass, looking out to the south-east to the slopes of Moel Siabod and down to the north-west into the deep shadows of rock architecture above the Afon Nant Peris.

At this time a small inn had for many years stood at the lower pass, where the Pen-y-Gwryd Hotel now stands. John Roberts of Pen-y-Bryn, Llanberis, was the first landlord there and the place attracted numerous of the early foot travellers to Snowdonia. The track for pedestrians which crossed Llanberis Pass was very rough and the traveller "had to pick his steps as he could with difficulty and suspicion, the path being irregular and rough and full of quagmires".

The Holyhead Road was made between Bettws-y-coed, Capel Curig and Bangor in the early years of the nineteenth century and so began the popularity of holidays in wildest Wales, albeit for only a select band of scholars and travellers initially. It was not many years later, however, that the steep and winding road was made through Llanberis Pass, between the small inn at Pen-y-Gwryd and Llanberis. In 1848 a small inn was built on the wild spot where only two heaps of stones had stood previously. It did not attract any quantity of mountain visitors (Pen-y-Gwryd claiming the lion's share due to its earlier establishment) until 1900, when Owen Rawson Owen came to Pen-y-Pass, to the Gorphwysfa Hotel.

The whitewashed cottages and the inn blossomed with a new facade and, in 1912, the new wing was built behind the old building, into the hillside amid huge, tumbled boulders. The upper floor accommodated a row of small bedrooms to house comfortably the many climbers who soon came to Pen-y-Pass. Below were the Rawson Owen's study and two large and well-equipped kitchens.

Among the group of notable climbers who came to Pen-y-Pass was Geoffrey Winthrop Young, one of the greatest mountaineers the world has ever seen. A scholar and poet, he was, too, a fine cragsman and climber upon many of the hardest mountain courses of Europe. He it was who explained the swing in popularity among mountaineers from Pen-y-Gwryd to Pen-y-Pass by listing the advantages of the latter – among them being "the highest roosting place in the island" where the mountaineer was "lodged upon the rim of space". Twenty minutes extra road walking were saved at both ends of the day by staying at Pen-y-Pass. The indescribable beauties viewed from Gorphwysfa were important, too; "the perfect mountain pyramid of Crib Goch" stands at the very door of the hotel rising in splendid (and apparent) isolation in front of the view whether dusted with early autumn snow or red-brown on hot June mornings when unseen lakes sparkle with promise. For Geoffrey Winthrop Young the finest mountain profile known to him was the "uprush of the Gallt-y-Wenallt ridge from the flat basin of Nant Gwynant" as seen a short distance down the road towards Pen-y-Gwryd.

In those quiet days of Edwardian elegance, at the evening of an era, the mountains of Snowdonia looked almost the same as today but the atmosphere of mountaineering and mountaineers has changed. The handful of scholars, engineers and athletes grew round themselves at the regular Easter meets more of like mind and we can read that "the meets of the halcyon years came to represent an almost ideal social fabric; and their recollection survives with us, apart in memory..."

A traverse of the entire Snowdon Horseshoe in conditions of snow and ice without taking one's hands from the pockets (done first by Professor Norman Collie), the race down to Pen-y-pass from the summit of Lliwedd in darkness after the day's climbing was done – a time of forty-three minutes was once recorded – and many, many more interesting doings were regularly undertaken, symbolic of the unique, imaginative and scholarly crowd before the Great War. It is sad to realise that so many of the colourful climbers who frequented the home of the Rawson Owens at that time never returned from the war. Of the few who did come back George Leigh Mallory died upon Everest in 1924 and Geoffrey Winthrop Young returned with one leg. It was he who subsequently did so many great ascents in the Alps with the aid of a duralumin artificial leg, reaching summits of considerable difficulty which included the Grepon, the Weisshorn and, his last Alpine top, the Zinal Rothorn in company with Marcus Heywood and Joseph Knubel, the former being one of the younger generation of Pen-y-Pass climbers before World War I, the latter one of the greatest of all Alpine professional guides who now lies at rest in the churchyard of St. Niklaus.

I never met G.W.Y. but corresponded with him in the years before his death in September, 1958. He was a genuine mountaineer and lover of all wild places; it was through him that the British Mountaineering Council came into being. Climbers of my acquaintance recall seeing those unique imprints upon the snow of Cwm Dyli, a footprint and the "slot" of his duralumin leg alternately, leading by Llyn Llydaw to the dark foot of Lliwedd. Had it not been for the loss of that leg G.W.Y. would most probably have been upon Everest in the twenties – it was, in fact, considered that he join the party in 1924 and go as far as the Base Camp, but he never went.

Owen Rawson Owen implanted his own strong personality upon
Pen-y-Pass, especially upon his Gorphwysfa Hotel there. Filled with
antiques and bric-a-brac the place was long a veritable treasure-house for
me. Not the least fascinating place was the barn above the road where
Owen stored his wonderful collection of phaetons, broughams and other
horse-drawn carriages smelling of old leather and leisurely days, of
drives to Bettys-y-coed railway station to fetch his climbing guests and
rattle them Pass-wards along the road which leaves the trees at Capel
Curig, skirts the twin lakes and grows ever wilder. Turning that last
corner Gorphwysfa comes into sight and the wind usually whistles, with
a rumble and sparks from horseshoes in the gathering gloom the
travellers would get down and breathe the fresh mountain air as the sun
flashed its last banners down Llanberis Pass and the grey-black cloud
curtains groped their sombre fingers about Crib Goch and all the
familiar hill-shapes.

With O.R.O.'s passing the carriages went, carried off on lorries down
Llanberis Pass to new homes far from their barn and the winds and
sunsets of Pen-y-Pass.

My last sight of Owen was on a wet August day in 1961. His tall frame
cast a shadow down the kitchen corridor as he went into his study, still a
great host of eighty-four, his Welsh voice singing out as always from the
depths of the "back-parts" of the house. In the later years he always
seemed to be in those "back-parts", though his characteristic voice was
often heard. The next year he died and a slab of slate stands to his
memory upon a wall of the front porch; on it simply:

OWEN RAWSON OWEN
1877-1962
HOST OF PEN-Y-PASS
FOR 60 YEARS

Upon the opposite wall is a similar slab of slate to the memory of the
other great character of the place, erected there by Owen, his friend. It
reads:

GEOFFREY WINTHROP YOUNG
1876-1958
POET AND MOUNTAINEER

Gorphwysfa Hotel was sold by the Vaynol Estate in the autumn of 1967 to the Youth Hostels Association of England and Wales. It is now a popular hostel in the YHA's top grade. The old iron shed which came from one of the Snowdon mines and was inhabited by Oscar Eckenstein and his friends for some years before and after World War I has been replaced by the large self-service restaurant.

Never again, to quote G.W.Y., will "the roar of Mrs. Owen's fandango on the dinner-gong" be heard across the head of the Pass at evening, but those skies, those northward vistas, remain – "down between the cliffs of Llanberis Pass, dark with eddying cloud or gorgeous with sunset, for perpetual evening company". He forecast the change at Gorphwysfa to meet the changing demands of a wider variety of visitors, demands generally less romantic and cultivated. He, too, saw the vistas from the head of the Pass unchanging – "vivid with blue tarn and crystal quartz, with snow-shield and frost-frond in the sunlight, or remote and mysterious under a gloom of cloud".

From the windows of O.R.O.'s new wing of 1912 one looks Anglesey-wards at evening, the light which twelve hours before lit up frontally the ribs and ridges and curving crest of Llechog above Nant Peris now shines from low-down beyond, throwing up the hill-shapes of the Pass as bold and solid masses. Above, the illuminated sky is bright with cloud-less duck-egg-blue or afire with blood-red banners of small cloud from over the sea. The levels of Anglesey and the waters beyond are not quite visible from here but one often imagines that they are, where some changing cloud-isle rests momentarily in the lowest nick of the converging slopes of the Snowdon massif and the Glyders. At such times it is hard to believe that G.W.Y. and his climbing friends are not being entertained in the smoking-room below by O.R.O. as he climbs round the chair-back, a feat that no-one else succeeded in repeating in a quarter of a century.

Chapter 4

EXPLORING ANGLESEY

The Menai Straits – Pre-history – Penmynydd and the Tudors – Penmon Priory –
Lighthouses – Power from Wylfa Head – Northernmost Wales.

Map: Ordnance Survey "Landranger" (1:50,000) Sheet 114 (Anglesey).

The sky is always blue over Anglesey, the sun always seems to shine
that way. Maybe those two statements are not entirely correct, but it
does so often seem that the low-lying, rectangular island across the
Menai Straits has fair weather when the mountains of Snowdonia are
experiencing low cloud and rain. My first encounters with the island are
remembered as long, enticing views down the Nant Ffrancon Pass as we
drove northwards from the dark clouds on Tryfan and the black faces of
the Glyders, down towards Bangor. The wind and rain had beat on the
road up from Capel Curig and now we went down towards Bethesda,
the Menai Straits sparkling brilliant blue in the distance and the greens
of Anglesey beckoned beyond, below an azure sky.

The name Anglesey is of Norse origin and means "the Island of the
Bend", the "Bend" being the twisting natural waterway of the Menai
Straits. It is an isle of ancient rocks, very ancient – in fact, Pre-Cambrian
(the oldest known rocks) and worn down low by agents of erosion over
the vast aeons of time and grooved by the passage of ice in the
Pleistocene period into shallow, parallel valleys and intervening ridges.
These run roughly between north-east and south-west, the best example
being the shallow vale occupied by Malltraeth Marsh. A deeper vale was
flooded by the sea to form the "moat of Anglesey", the Menai Straits of
the present time. It is most interesting to note how closely the next
shallow vale to the north (drained by the Afon Braint) follows the line of
the Menai Straits. Look at a map of Anglesey and see how all the main
streams run in a general direction from north-east to south-west.

The Menai Straits do bend or curve, especially at their narrowest, midway along their length. The water is less than five fathoms deep for much of this length and so is not of much use to any but the smallest of vessels. When Archbishop Baldwin of Canterbury and Ranulph de Glanville led the Third Crusade to drive the Saracens out of the Holy Land after the fall of Jerusalem in 1187 the party had to ford the Menai Straits to reach Anglesey, traditionally near the church of Llantysilio. Here came Saint Tysilio in the sixth century – in the "Age of Saints" – and set up his teaching on an islet reached by crossing a causeway (map reference: 552717). Subsequently, ferries carried men, animals and objects across the strait, ferries like the Garth ferry which operated from the end of Bangor pier.

In 1826 Thomas Telford's beautiful suspension bridge was opened and the mail coach route from London to Ireland via Holyhead was completed. Mail coaches ran over the bridge, carrying men and mails for many years, but eventually Robert Stephenson's fine and gigantic Britannia tubular bridge carrying the railway to Holyhead was built between 1846 and 1850. What a wonderful structure this bridge is, far bigger than a distant view of it would at first suggest. The history of the building of the bridge and its virtual destruction by fire and subsequent re-building in the 1970s makes fascinating reading.

At the other end of the bridge, where it rests on Anglesey's rocks, there is the church of Llanfair P.G. or Llanfairpwllgwyngyll, the shortened forms of the well-known village which boasts the longest place-name in the world. Just below the church we gain the sea-worn boulders on the edge of the strait and here stands the monument to Lord Nelson, a fine statue of the man atop a four-sided base. The old door to the interior of the base has been broken, as have the wooden steps which once went up to the balcony around the figure. Of course, there is an even more notable monument not far away across the Holyhead road. This one is the Anglesey Column which is 90 feet high and is topped by the bronze statue of the Marquis of Anglesey of Plas Newydd who commanded the cavalry at Waterloo. The spiral staircase leads one to the balcony, from where wonderful views of the mainland mountains and Anglesey and the water between can be obtained.

Until some years ago the wooden man-o'-war H.M.S. *Conway* was anchored in the Menai Straits and used as a cadet training school for the

Merchant Navy. While going for a refit at Liverpool she went aground just west of Telford's suspension bridge on the mainland shore and was wrecked. Subsequently the timbers got on fire and the beautiful old ship was totally destroyed. Today the Merchant Navy school occupies a fine mansion overlooking the Menai Straits.

Plas Newydd, the home of the Marquis of Anglesey stands on the Anglesey shore of the Straits two miles west of the Britannia Bridge, where the channel turns to run in a north-south direction for some distance. It is now a National Trust property and open to the public in summer.

As for men of the distant past, Anglesey was a stronghold of the Druids who were once thought to be priests come over the sea from Ireland. Anglesey was thought by an eighteenth-century authority to be the last refuge rather than the headquarters of Druids in Britain. Unfortunately they were forbidden by their own laws to put their knowledge down in writing so that all that remains is what classical writers refer to, and what can be deduced from Celtic folklore. The low-lying island was naturally very attractive to man in pre-historic times, a fertile area and mild when compared with the mountains of the mainland behind. One only has to look at the Ordnance Survey map to note the great number of pre-historic remains hereabouts. It would need a whole book of this size to do justice to even the best-known pre-historic remains of Anglesey so that I can do no more here than whet the appetite and refer to one or two of these interesting relics of very different days on this island of Mon or Mona or "yr ynys dywyll" (island dark with trees) or "Island of the Bend" or twisting and watery strait.

A strain of people of Iberian origin populated the western extremities of Britain and the only monuments to these people now left in North Wales are the dolmens (or burial places using great stones, or megaliths), of which about twenty survive in Anglesey. The best preserved is the Chambered Cairn of Bryn Celli Ddu (map reference: 507701) not far from the Menai Straits. The monument can be reached easily, at the end of a long, straight farm track from the lane to Llanddaniel-Fab. It was erected about 1,500 B.C. for communal burial and is similar to others at New Grange, near Drogheda, Eire, and Kercado in Brittany. This relic, as much as any other, is worthy of a visit to wonder at the great skill and imagination of the builders. It is normally open to the public.

The chambered cairn of Bryn Celli Ddu, near Llanddaniel-Fab, southern Anglesey

An older burial chamber occupies the top of a west-facing headland called Barclodiad y Gawres, near Rhosneigr (map reference: 329707). It dates from the New Stone Age, between 2,500 and 1,900 B.C. and was erected, like the former one, for the communal burial of the dead. There is a chamber and passage within a round and dome-topped cairn, and there are stones bearing the fine spiral and chevron patterns typical of the period. This antiquity is also normally open to the public. The situation, though less dramatic, reminds me of the ruined cairn above high cliffs on Barra's western side.

Look at the map of the island and see the great number of pre-historic remains marked – burial chambers, chambered cairns (often the same thing), standing stones and earthworks. One of the most accessible stones is that standing close by the road north-east of Llanfaelog (map reference: 356746) and marked as an "Inscribed Stone". Who were the men who erected and decorated such a stone? That is the mystery and here lies one of the charms of the island. Caer-y-Twr is a hill-fort with a stone rampart upon the 700 feet summit of Holyhead Mountain and here again the precise date of this remain is uncertain.

Down below the north-western slopes of this upland are the vertical and overhanging cliffs called Craig Gogarth, overlooking Gogarth Bay, where many new climbing routes have been opened up since 1965, almost all of them demanding a very high standard of cragsmanship in a lovely, sea-facing and sun-catching position.

Anglesey has its share of more recent history, too. The best example of this is set in Anglesey's pastoral heart, a short way eastwards from Llangefni at a place called Penmynydd.

Plas Penmynedd, near Llangefni, birthplace of Owen Tudor

Between Llangefni and the little village of Penmynydd we pass the end of a farm drive leading to the ancient mansion of Plas Penmynydd (map reference: 496752). If we walk along this drive towards the old house, a lane bounded by "bocage" banks which are such familiar boundaries in south-west Wales, Cornwall and Brittany, the abundant flora of spring and early summer will be noticed – celandine, primrose, violet and dandelion above a ditch of clear water blocked by fresh-leaved watercress. Gorse blazes on hedgerows and right across Anglesey's heart. This island's gorse is truly a spectacle, especially in April and May. An eminent modern botanist has stated that it is "about the most buttery, luscious gorse in the world".

The tall chimneys of the mansion are now visible with a dark backing of coniferous trees in the garden. Soon we reach it, a plain building with a moulding on the wall adjoining the house with the date "1576" on it. Here was born Owen Tudor, of Welsh yeoman stock and a Welshman destined to influence and alter the course of subsequent British history, who brought to the English throne his own humble family name.

But let us now go to the old church of Saint Gredifael (who was brother of Saint Llechid) which was founded over 1,300 years ago in "the Age of the Celtic Saints". The first stone church was erected here in the twelfth century and the present structure was built in the fourteenth century (map reference: 517750). Adjoining the nave on the northern side is a simple addition gained by a Gothic arch, built at the same time as the porch over the main door in the fifteenth century. Inside this addition – the Tudor Chapel – is the tomb of Gronw Fychan and his wife Myfanwy supporting alabaster effigies of the pair, badly chipped by people of past ages taking away a small fragment of the alabaster in the belief that it could be used for medicinal purposes to cure disease. The tomb is dated 1385, so the bodies must have been moved to this place when the chapel was erected some years later.

This Gronw Fychan was the first cousin of Owen Glendower (or Owain Glyndwr) and uncle of Owen Tudor to whom I have already referred as being born at Plas Penmynydd. Fychan was a friend of the Black Prince and the first Welshman to be appointed Constable of Beaumaris Castle, in 1382, but was drowned in Kent not long after his appointment.

A small window in the east wall of the chapel contains very old glass bearing a picture of the red rose of the Tudors, while the family's coat of arms can be found carved in stone upon the south wall of the chancel. Another interesting feature are the fleur-de-lis carved on the ends of the pews, and for a very good reason.

Katherine de Valois was married to King Henry V and was widowed at the early age of twenty-one. After fighting under Henry at Agincourt, Owen Tudor became Clerk of the Wardrobe to the widowed queen at Windsor. His secret marriage to Katherine was kept a secret for fourteen years, as were the three sons born to her. In 1436 she became ill after the birth of a daughter and the secret was no more. Owen was thrown into Newgate Prison and Katherine died.

Penmynydd church, Anglesey, containing relics of the early Tudors

Owen escaped from captivity and went home to Wales. However, he was recaptured and put again into Newgate Prison. He again escaped to Wales and Henry VI finally acknowledged him as the rightful husband of the dead queen, and his sons born to her were accepted as legitimate. And so, after many eventful years, the seventy-six year old Owen Tudor led a Royalist army against the Yorkists and was defeated at Mortimer's Cross, Herefordshire, in 1461 and beheaded in Hereford Market Place. His grandson had been born at Pembroke Castle in June 1456, and was the Henry Tudor who defeated Richard III at the Battle of Bosworth to become Henry VII, the first Tudor king.

On the death of Henry VII the mummified remains of his grandmother, Katherine de Valois, were exhumed and kept on view in Westminster Abbey until well into George III's reign in the eighteenth century. Today the pew-ends in Penmynydd Church commemorate the French wife-queen of Owen Tudor of Plas Penmynydd, a woman who was a member of the French Royal House before marrying her first husband.

Near Anglesey's easternmost headland, Penmon Point, is another area with strong historic associations. It centres upon Penmon Priory (map reference: 631807) which was originally a Celtic monastery founded in the seventh century.

Saint Seiriol came here in the sixth century and probably lived in the oval chamber close by the well which takes his name, just behind the present priory ruins. The lower portion of the chamber over the lovely well of clear spring water may possibly date from Saint Seiriol's time; the upper portion consists of bricks and mortar of the eighteenth century. The well was used originally for baptism.

The ruins of the priory date largely from the thirteenth century, once forming the range on the south side of the priory cloister. They were erected when the old Celtic monastery was re-organised as an Augustinian monastery. On the first floor was the refectory, below it was the cellar and above it, on the second floor, the dormitory. At the eastern end there is the kitchen and warming room, added in the sixteenth century. The church behind is still used as a place of worship, being partly rebuilt and of cruciform layout, with an early Norman nave and south transept. Across the lane stands the imposing dovecote, dating from about 1600. It is a square structure with domed vault and hexagonal cupola. The eggs were collected from the nesting boxes lining the insides of the four walls by means of a ladder supported on the top of the great stone pillar which occupies the centre of the dovecote, with projecting steps spiralling to its top.

It is not really understood why this great dovecote was erected as late as 1600 for by that time the priory would have few permanent residents and the requirements for meat and eggs as supplied by the pigeons here

would likewise be relatively small. Perhaps they were sent to neighbouring districts of Anglesey and the mainland.

In the deer park a little way to the north stands the Penmon Cross which
dates from about A.D. 1100 and has an elaborately carved rectangular
shaft depicting the Temptation of Saint Anthony.

From the cross-roads at Llanallgo overlooking Anglesey's eastern coast
(map reference: 504854) one can look down to the north towards Dulas
Bay and the rocky islet of Ynys Dulas. Upon this islet stand the remains
of a tower erected for the safety of sailors shipwrecked off-shore. At the
mansion set in finely wooded parkland at Dulas lived a wealthy woman
who saw fit to have this tower erected, with supplies of food, water and
fuel for anyone who should be marooned there. Today the place lies
neglected, a memory of an act of great charity to those in trouble on the
sea. And from that same cross-roads viewpoint one can look to Moelfre,
a mile down the road to the north. On October 26th, 1859, the merchant
ship *Royal Charter* headed for Liverpool on the last part of its long
journey from Australia with a cargo of gold worth £450,000 on board.
While rounding Anglesey a severe gale developed, referred to at that
time as "a cyclone". Holyhead harbour was the obvious port for which
to make for shelter but there was no room there as the *Great Eastern* was
anchored and so the captain of the *Royal Charter* sought the lee shore off
Moelfre. Eventually the vessel was wrecked here and 446 lives were lost.
It is recorded that for a long time afterwards bodies were washed
ashore, as many as seventeen being washed up in one night. The dead
were buried in Llanallgo churchyard. Much of the cargo of gold was
recovered in the form of dust, ingots and coins as the mahogany boxes
in which it was contained burst open on the sea-bed off-shore. The lost
gold has ever-after been the object of salvage operations but these have
to date been unsuccessful and the sea will surely have strewn and buried
the treasure in the past century.

The coast around Anglesey, especially on the west and north is busy
with shipping in and out of Liverpool. Its coastline is, then, a great
hazard and, as such, is well marked with light beacons and lighthouses.
There are lifeboat stations at Holyhead, Beaumaris and Moelfre. The
lighthouse on the rocky islet of South Stack is well known to most
people visiting Anglesey. One reaches it beyond the end of the lane
which winds westwards from Holyhead. High cliffs fall to the Irish Sea

beyond, loud with the call of sea birds and there, far below, stands the rock-isle known as South Stack. The lighthouse always appears white and fresh, its light of 2,500,000 candelas intensity (equivalent to 2,425,000 English candles) being exhibited 197 feet above mean sea level. The light flashes white every ten seconds and has a range of 20 sea miles but is obscured to the northward by the islet of North Stack. By taking the steep, airy and winding stair down to the new bridge over the sea-plunging cleft one has a fine view of the cliffs and sea birds and sucking seaweed steeps beneath. In wild weather, with grey seas running before westerly gusts beneath a torn sky scudding in from the ocean this situation typifies the spirit of many a mid-Victorian romantic painting.

Away to the north-east, round the corner in Gogarth Bay, are the soaring sea cliffs now called Craig Gogarth and opened-up by climbers, including Peter Crew and Joe Brown, since 1965. Here, the advantages of a low-lying cliff on a sunny island make the cliff most attractive when the grey cliffs of highest Snowdonia are running with rain and darkened by deep cloud-layers.

The group of rocks called Ynysoedd y Moelrhoniaid lie two miles off north-western Anglesey and are better known as The Skerries. They rise less than fifty feet above sea level and are a great danger to shipping, marked by the lighthouse with a round, white tower with a red band. It is 75 feet tall and the 4,000,000 candle-power light is exhibited 119 feet above mean sea level, the light flashes twice every ten seconds and is visible 17 sea miles in clear conditions.

On the north-eastern headland of Anglesey, called Point Lynas, stands the Lynas Lighthouse with its occulting light (longer periods of light than darkness) of 112,000 candelas visible to 17 sea miles. This peculiar building of rectangular and castellated shape is maintained by the Mersey Docks and Harbour Board. The walk out to the headland from Llaneilian has lovely views into little Porthyrysgaw, the shallow bay on the western side.

Between the north-western and north-eastern headlands of Anglesey the north coast ins-and-outs between rocky headlands and sandy bays like Cemaes and Cemlyn. Between these two beautiful bays stands Wylfa Head and when it was first suggested that a nuclear power station might be built on the lovely northern coast of Anglesey there was an understandable outcry from many quarters. With a similar power station being erected at Trawsfynydd at the heart of the Snowdonia National Park it was feared that many of the finest corners of North Wales would be ruined by a "rash" of such projects.

Work started on the power station in April, 1964 and was completed in 1968. Its construction produced much needed employment for local people.

Less than two miles to the north-east of Cemaes Bay stands Anglesey's northernmost headland upon which stands the prehistoric fortification called Dinas Gwynfor. Part of the steep cliffs here which drop to the north-east sea are now owned by the National Trust and so will retain their beauty indefinitely.

Telford's suspension bridge, from the Anglesey shore

Chapter 5

ABOVE THE MAWDDACH

The Mawddach Valley – Panorama Walk – Llwyn-onn Hill Farms -Shipbuilding – Sword Stones – Gold Mining – Water Supply

Route: Barmouth – Garn Gorllwyn – Bwlch y Llan – Bwlch Cymmaria – Bwlch y Rhiwgyr-Diffwys or Sylfaen – Barmouth

Distance: 14 miles or 7 miles

Grade: Strenuous

Starting Point: Barmouth (map reference: 613159)

Maps: Ordnance Survey "Landranger" (1:50,000) Sheet 124 (Dolgellau and Surrounding Area). Ordnance Survey "Outdoor Leisure" (1:25,000) Sheet 18 (Snowdonia – Harlech and Bala Area).

Though the River Mawddach rises in the high mountain-hollow called Waunygriafolen in the parish of Llanuwchllyn it is in the seven mile length of its tidal estuary that it is most beautiful and best known.

In the mountainous miles above ancient Llanelltyd Bridge the river tumbles wide and foaming through woodland and above famous Rhaeadr Mawddach (the Mawddach Falls) it drains an area of lonely hills. This region was once well populated by sheep farmers and their families but today, as throughout much of upland Wales, depopulation has virtually emptied these rolling hills and wide hollows. This is little-known Wales, off-the-beaten track Wales, and I am sure that few readers will have the good fortune to know this basin of the Upper Mawddach intimately. By the side of the river, just above Llanelltyd Bridge, are the ruins of Cymmer Abbey. These are now in the care of the Ministry of Works and should be visited. The abbey was founded in 1199 by the Cistercian order. The Cistercian way of life appealed to Welsh ways and temperament and numerous similar abbeys were founded in this country. The intention to extend the building eastwards from the river was never put into practice, though a tower was added in 1350.

Below Llanelltyd Bridge the sea takes hold of affairs, raising and lowering the level of the Mawddach every day. Once the estuary was filled by the sea, and more beautiful it was then, no doubt. The curving sandspit of Ro Wen, laid down by longshore sea currents in Cardigan Bay, has almost cut off the mouth of the estuary so that behind it lies an area of salt marsh, covered only at the highest tides. Elsewhere the rugged edge of the estuary is being smoothed out by the establishment of marshland, notably at the mouth of the Afon Dwynant by Glan-dwr, and above Bontddu.

It is not long ago that the drive down the sinuous road (the A496) skirting the northern shore of the estuary was an experience of mixed emotions-mixed by a combination of beauty and danger. The high, pennywort-colonised walls of Cambrian slate hemmed in and confined vehicles and one's driving difficulties allowed little time to see the lovely land.

Much of this route has now been improved – straightened, widened, opened-out. While this at first might sound like many other so-called "improvements" to roads, I think the sensible road-user will agree that the new and well-designed road has not spoilt the countryside hereabouts one bit, and gives the traveller a much better view of the estuary, the northern face of Cadair Idris beyond and, in limited measure, of the southern slopes of the Harlech Dome which descend on this northern side down to the Mawddach's shores.

I doubt if there is a more beautiful estuary in Britain; but go to the Mawddach and see for yourself if you have never been. The purpose of this chapter is not to proclaim beauty so much as to describe details of the lesser known hills above the Mawddach's northern shore, details of a land well loved and worth knowing.

Intimate knowledge of an area as beautiful as here unfailingly brings greater joy. I came here at six months of age and every return brings me closer to these slopes and sheep and clean, grey stones.

The steep little road leading out of Barmouth and up to the famous Panorama Walk (with its wide views over the Mawddach estuary to Cadair Idris, the Aran mountains and the Irish Sea) was once the only way into the town from Dolgellau. The lane led up by the Panorama Walk and then descended sharply through the trees to the mouth of the Afon Dwynant (which drains the Glan-dwr valley). In these trees, and not far below the Panorama Walk, are the ruins of an ancient inn called Bwlch-y-Goedloedd. It has long been vacant and used as a farm building though its walls still stand solid and its great chimney stack remains square above the encircling ivy.

The great poet Dafydd ap Gwilym stayed here at this inn in, or about, 1335 and is said to have arranged to meet separately about a dozen lovely Welsh girls one evening. Only when all the girls arrived together at the arranged point was his plot revealed and he quickly retreated to the shelter of his room in the Bwlch-y-Goedloedd.

The lane forks near the Panorama Walk, the direct, straight-ahead route climbing gently eastwards, then in half a mile it turns up steeply between rocks and ferns, overhung by mountain ash trees. It passes the derelict farmhouse of Llwyn-gloddaeth and so on to level grassland where wide views proclaim themselves on every side but the west. Steeply down are wall-enclosed fields and the ancient farm of Llwyn-onn Isaf.

The slopes slip on down to the Mawddach's shores, almost 700-feet below, ahead the lovely Glan-dwr valley leads the eye on to the distant summit of lonely Y Garn (2,063 feet), the Cairn. Round the next corner the hidden farmland comes to view, rising to the bracken-clothed and stone wall slopes that rear to the undulating crest of the main ridge, the ridge called Llawlech. This mountain arm curves south-westwards from the summit of distant Diffwys (2,462 feet) to tumble in stony confusion into the sea where Barmouth stands. Some of this steep ground overlooking the town, incidentally, was given to the Nation many years ago and constitutes the first property ever acquired by the National Trust. It is called Dinas Oleu, "The Fortress of Light".

Below us, if we stand at the highest point of Llwyn-onn Bach Mountain (1,550 feet) are the farmlands of Sylfaen and Llwyn-onn.

Diffwys ((2,462') from Craig-y-Grit on the Llawlech Ridge

Llwyn-onn is really three mountain farms. There is Llwyn-onn Isaf (the Farm below the Ash Grove) already mentioned far down in the trees; there is Llwyn-onn Uchaf (The Farm above the Ash Grove), a farm once owned by Sir Clayton Russon and recently modernised; and there is Llwyn-onn Bach (The Little Ash Grove). Here formerly lived Mr and Mrs Hughie Jones.

Mr Jones was born here, the son of a sheep farmer who came originally from Llanbedr. I have a special affection for this place and these people. I came to live here for one bright summer long ago, having completed a year's study at a Farm Institute. Time has mellowed those long days beneath wide Welsh skies and a handful of sharp memories remain – of scything bracken among the fly-filled woods of Llwyn-onn Isaf, of loading the bracken onto a low cart and helping to move it to the barn near the house for winter bedding for the cows; memories of snatching an odd cartload of sweet-smelling meadow hay between days of alternating wind and rain, of dipping sheep near Bryn Annas with Harry Williams, his uncle and Mr Jones.

Then there was the day of intense, sultry heat when thunder rolled from mountain to mountain ever nearer as we, with Mr Hugh Jones senior, loaded hay from the fields above the farm and took it down to the barn, and back for another load. During the evening the storm broke overhead, thunder roared in the yard and the air was tense with electricity as our paraffin lamp flickered on the living-room table and the rain poured down from the living night sky.

Every morning and evening we walked to Tyn-y-Maes to milk the Welsh Black cows and returned between the high banks of sloe, fern, dog roses, the last foxgloves and bracken, with full buckets. Then Mrs Jones set to work to separate the cream and twice a week she made butter in her hand churn. Every morning seemed fine that long summer, and each morning I looked out of my tiny, south-facing window and took in the fresh mountain air and the views of Cadair Idris, the Mawddach, the distant Arans and, leaning right out of the window, I could see as far as the breasts of lovely hill country culminating in Sylfaen mountain. On some days faint wreaths of mist rested on those summits, on others weak sunlight picked out the sheep grazing there.

Mrs Mary Jones at Llwyn-Onn Bach, 1965

Long walks with the dogs to the sheep on the high grazing grounds seem to have been invariably in mist or drizzle, as on a particularly dark day when Mr Jones and his father and I walked up to the remote enclosure of "mountain" called Ffridd Maes-y-Clawdd and there we sorted lambs and ewes, checking the ewes for maggots and foot-rot. The dogs worked well, I recall, that day and Mot, though old, did his share. Young Tim bounced up and sown the steep, rock-strewn slopes like a mountain hare. Dell was the favourite, an able and intelligent bitch who never had a family. I remember her as a fluffy, lovable puppy at Cae Cam in Anglesey.

From Llwyn-onn Bach a narrow lane winds down past "Grace's Well" and Llwyn-onn Isaf to the little hamlet of Cutiau. When the Watkins retired from Llwyn-onn Isaf in 1952 that property was purchased by the Joneses, leased for many years to the Inter Varsity Club (Birmingham Branch). Now it is owned by Mrs Jones's nephew and family so continues in the same family these forty years. It is a substantial farmhouse on the lines of many which lie upon the flanks of the Merionethshire mountains, having massive chimney stacks and walls at least a yard thick. The date of 1689 over the front door may be the date when it was built to replace the much older house (now a ruin) which stands up the slope nearer Llwyn-onn Bach. It is modelled upon this older dwelling with few alterations save an increase in size.

Shaded beneath old trees upon the south-facing slope is the little settlement of Cutiau, a collection of cottages, derelict farms, one or two

Cadair Idris from Llyn-Onn Bach, across the Mawddach Estuary

more imposing houses and the old chapel. About 1825 the Congregationalists began the teaching of their doctrines hereabouts, led by Evan Evans of Llangollen. In a letter dated November 16th, 1826 three senior members of the twenty-strong congregation asked this man to be their official Minster and stated that "regarding your sustenance, we of Cutiau promise to collect eight pounds a year". Evan Evans accepted and was ordained on May 23rd, 1827 at the lovely "Chapel in the Valley".

Later a large chapel was built in the centre of Barmouth and the little chapel remained to succour the inhabitants of the farms and cottages in the hills around. Mr Jones recalls his childhood days when dozens of men, women and children gathered, and there were teas and parties and meetings. Slowly the mountain farms emptied, few of those that remained contained young people and today the beautifully sited chapel has a congregation numbering, it is jokingly said, "four when they all attend". Still, though, the building remains beneath its tree canopy and the sheep crop the grass between the gravestones, and the waters of the Afon Dwynant still tumble noisily in the valley's rocky bed below.

Shipbuilding

Shipbuilding flourished in the Mawddach until the last century, when the coming of the railway in 1867 and the discovery that timber grown by the Mawddach developed dry rot ended this industry in a relatively short time. Another cause of de-population at Cutiau was the building of the new road and bridge over the river here. This prevented vessels entering the creek to unload grain for the flour mill and other provisions. Vessel-loads were then loaded and unloaded onto the banks of the estuary. The owner of this ground issued proceedings against the local people, who contested the case and won their battle in a London court. The owner was enraged and gave his tenants notice to quit and soon very few properties hereabouts remained inhabited. One house worthy of note here is Bod Owen, overlooking the creek just mentioned. This was the home of Major H. W. Tilman, one of the world's greatest mountain explorers. Besides being the leader of the team which made the first ascent of Nanda Devi in 1936, he was leader of the 1938 British Everest Expedition, and took up sailing to his mountains in later years in a converted Bristol pilot cutter, mountains in Norway, Patagonia, Greenland and Antarctica.

Up the airy mountains above Llwyn-onn is another world, a world between 650 and 1,900 feet above sea level. And up here one used to often meet Major Tilman and his dogs, when he wasn't climbing or sailing abroad. The grass gives way to the bracken and, near the summit ridge, the bilberry and stagshorn moss takes over. Buzzards fly by, and choughs; while below cry the sheep. The high, dry-stone walls lead straight up these mountains to the ridge, dividing Llwyn-onn Isaf from Bach, and Bach from Sylfaen. On the steep and tumbled rocks, hardly screes, of upper Llwyn-on Bach Mountain I remember building a dry-stone cairn on a warm, still September evening in 1953 to commemorate the first ascent of Everest only three months before. Strange to relate I have never since been able to find the cairn again – is it still there, or have the sheep knocked it down?

Upon the summit of Diffwys on Coronation Day in 1953 a great fire blazed in the night sky. It is related that Major Tilman and friends were responsible for this unique, and remote, celebration a little while before my cairn-building.

Two of the dogs were with me on that lovely evening. Mot, old and very deaf but still a good friend, struggled up the stony slope after me. Ahead and rushing to the sunset over the summit ridge streaked Tim, the young dog of the farm in those days. He always seemed a happy dog, with a long tongue that dripped heavily after exertion, and his long wiry coat collected blood-sucking ticks from the bracken in summer. Now both these dogs have passed to their Happy Hunting Ground.

Along the lane beyond Llwyn-onn is the large farm called Sylfaen, long the home of the Williams. Beyond Sylfaen, at the 700 feet level, the lane winds along to the north-east, under Llawlech's slopes, and above the long-ruined farm of Golodd. I have often thought of this place as the original "Old House" as sung by John MacCormack. Yes, long empty and silent, the family has moved on, the children never to return. In fact, the roof has gone and a hawthorn tree grows in the centre of the house, a hooded crow's nest in its impenetrable branches. The chimney is, as in all the farmhouses of these hills, a tremendously strong affair of native rock, complete with a bread oven where a fire of wood was lit and when the stones within had become red-hot the fire was removed and the dough placed inside to bake. The outbuildings are still in good repair and used, with the land, as part of the Sylfaen property.

The old stable on the track leading down into Sylfaen Wood

Beyond Golodd the track continues to an iron gate, by the side of which is the Roman Well. Here, there are steps down to the water lying in its shaded, fern-overhung bower. It is water of the purest type, always cool and soft. Mr Jones used to relate how ailing children were brought up here long ago to drink this sparkling water and how many sickly infants have been cured. Going through the iron gate we proceed on towards a place where the walls on either hand converge and form a "drive" towards Diffwys's nearest flanks. Just before this "drive" is entered look for the Roman stable on the right-hand side of the track, a partly-roofed enclosure where men and horses traditionally took rest and shelter *en-route* for the coast. Huge blocks of slate form the roof and high stone walls form the enclosure. This structure may well date from Roman times for why should these tremendous roof slabs deteriorate in two millenia?

Away to the south-east, upon the top of the damp shoulder stretching towards the Mawddach, and about half a mile distant is the renowned Cerrig y Cledd. This is, literally, the Sword Stones. Here stands a large boulder upon the shoulder of moor, split vertically by the action of frost over the centuries. On two faces of the split rock are the "carvings" of an ancient leaf-shaped British sword two feet nine inches in length. What is the origin of this remarkable and remote mountain feature?

Firstly, two traditions. One is that here at Cae'r Cleddau – the Field of Swords – the last battle was fought between the Romans and the Welsh. A treaty was finally agreed upon and the Welsh threw a sword into the air as a pledge of faith. The sword landed upon this rock and split it, leaving the impressions we still see today. The second tradition asserts that a Welshman met a Roman soldier near this spot close to the Roman road over the hills. A fight took place and the Roman was killed. Setting off homewards with the newly acquired sword he soon saw a group of Roman soldiers searching for their comrade. The Welshman plunged the sword into the ground to avoid detection. The earth grew round the sword, turned to rock and finally the rock was eroded onto the surface where frost split it open where the sword's impression remains.

Be these traditions as they may it would seem to me that here is a bubble formed in the ancient Cambrian rock, sword-shaped by chance, and now exposed by the action of frost. Cerrig y Cledd is well worth a visit, an object for a lovely walk up from Barmouth or the Mawddach's shores. Unfortunately in the last thirty years a dense planting of coniferous forest has engulfed the site and makes location of Cerrig y Cledd difficult. It is marked on both scales of maps of the area as an antiquity.

The ancient route from Bontddu forks at the Roman Well, one arm climbing steeply over the Llawlech ridge to reach 1,500 feet at Bwlch y Rhiwgyr. Going down towards Bontddu from the Roman Well we soon reach the ruins of an ancient house on the left. This was once an inn on this lonely stretch of track, a welcome hostelry, no doubt, to many travellers in former days. Like Bwlch-y-Goedloedd it lies in ruins, but more so on account of a bleaker situation and, maybe, greater antiquity.

Mr Hugh Jones senior used to recall the long tramp over Llawlech by men living at Dyffryn Ardudwy and Llanbedr. Each Sunday evening they would cross this high ridge by the traversing path clearly seen from this valley in fine weather. It crossed the smooth hillside to the north at about 1,700 feet above sea level. These men were returning to a week's work in the gold mines near Bontddu, where they lodged in shacks, and would return the eight miles home on the Saturday with their small wages. Work was so hard to come by eighty or one hundred years ago that any honest source of income, and type of hard labour, any distance to trudge to get it, was welcomed by those men who were not fishermen or sheep farmers on a sufficiently large scale.

Gold Mining

This is the only place in the British Isles where gold has been mined in any quantity. The whole of the upland between the Mawddach and the Vale of Ffestiniog is composed of Cambrian rocks, the second oldest geological era known to man. This is the largest exposure of such rock in these islands and in them occur what are known as "secondary metalliferous lodes". These lodes are impregnated with such things as sulphides of iron, arsenic and free gold. The chief occurrences are in the Clogau shales but working for gold has extended into the older Barmouth Grits further to the north.

But for the fact that a number of Royal wedding rings are made from Merionethshire gold most of the world would be ignorant that this precious metal occurs hereabouts. It has been suggested that the Romans discovered gold near Bontddu, above the Mawddach, but there is no evidence to support this tradition.

As far as I can ascertain gold was first found here in 1834 but due to the amount of ridicule this engendered no mines were opened until 1847. At one time there were over twenty-four mines in operation on the southern slopes of the Harlech Dome. Many of these mines never produced any return, though the discovery of gold at the Clogau mine (a little further to the north of Bontddu) was followed by something of a "rush". Many companies sprang up, expensive machinery was installed, and the area buzzed with life and excitement. However, only two mines were really successful. The first was the Gwynfynydd Mine, far up the Mawddach valley near Ganllwyd, and the first gold was procured in 1864. Between 1888 and 1890 £35,000's worth was extracted, but thereafter little of value was brought out up to 1916, when it was closed. This gold contained more silver than most and was consequently of a paler colour than Bontddu gold.

At the Clogau Mine gold was found in 1860 and in 1865 £22,575 was paid in dividends. This mine was closed in 1910. Despite numerous efforts to open up the industry again it has never again become important. At an enquiry held at Dolgellau in 1930 an authority stated that "mining in this district must be a highly venturesome business" because of the sporadic nature of the pockets of gold ore.

From the top of the Llawlech ridge above the Roman Well one can look down into the wild hollow containing Llyn Bodlyn, a little lake enlarged by the building of an impounding wall to raise its level by ten feet in 1890. This is Barmouth's main source of water, covers 40 acres and holds 102 million gallons above the draw-off level. The Afon Ysgethin runs out of the lake and is crossed by the winding miner's track already mentioned at a place called Pont Scethin.

Across the broad vale to the north is the rounded bulk of Moelfre (1,932 feet) crowned by its ancient cairn, probably a prehistoric shrine. Round to the right, beneath the north-facing flank of Diffwys, are crags overlooking Llyn Bodlyn where a memorial tablet reminds the traveller of a youth who lost his life while climbing there in search of bird's eggs. The birds of the colony, ravens and choughs and an occasional buzzard, still nest where he fell so long ago.

The lonely track winds up from Pont Scethin and, not far up the slope from the river, is another memorial tablet. It is a grave-like tablet of slate to the memory of Janet Haigh, the mother of a former Bishop of Winchester. This lady walked this route from Talybont on the coast to Penmaenpool regularly well into her eighty-fourth year "despite failing sight and stiffening joints". It was erected here in 1953 by her son and at the base of the tablet are the appropriate works "Courage Traveller".

From the top of the pass we can return, as I have often returned, along Llawlech's ridge-top towards the south-west and descend to Sylfaen and on to Llwyn-onn as the brilliant sundown lights fade on Cadair Idris across the estuary. And I rush on and down to Llwyn-onn Bach, to the welcome that always awaited me, for Mrs Hughie Jones was my aunt.

The Route

1. A fine walk can be had by walking up the ridge-end from Barmouth, over the 870 feet summit of Garn Gorllwyn and so on up and down, over the rocky hillocks and into the numerous rushy hollows which lie on the ridge. A Roman route crosses the pass called Bwlch y Llan, between Llanber on the coast and Bontddu on the Mawddach. A short

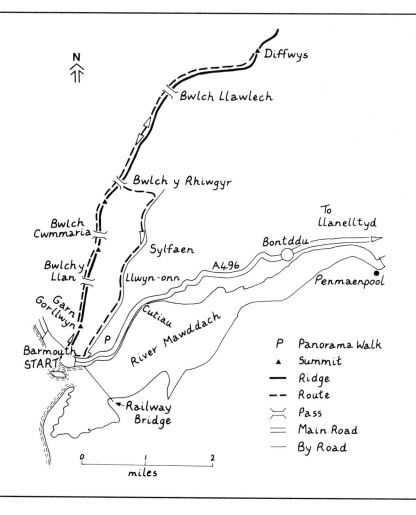

way down the track from the top of the pass, on the western (Llanaber) side, are the remains of a fortress established by the Romans to protect their route. A section of fine, dry-stone walling over two hundred feet long and a moat are the best-preserved of these ruins. It may be that these are the remains of Pennant's "Castell Dinas y Gortin".

2. Proceeding up the ridge we go first over the summit of Llwynonn Isaf Mountain, descend into Bwlch Cwmmaria and climb the slaty ridge to the higher top of Llwyn-onn Bach. From this breezy top we can look out on a clear day to the far end of the Lleyn peninsula and lovely Bardsey Island thirty miles distant, to the south the northern cliffs of Cadair Idris hang above the foothills which slide, wooded, into the Mawddach. Ahead, to the north-east, is the wild land of the Harlech Dome, rugged hills of Cambrian rocks; this area between the Mawddach estuary and the Vale of Ffestiniog is composed of the largest exposure of Cambrian rocks in the British Isles.

The ridge curves on, over a top of 1,689 feet, down to Bwlch y Rhiwgyr, up to the 1,930 feet summit of Sylfaen Mountain and so on down to Bwlch Llawlech and, finally, gently on and up to the summit of distant Diffwys.

3. We can either continue along this long watershed all the way to Diffwys summit, then retrace our steps as far as Bwlch y Rhiwgyr (map reference: 628200), or . . .

3a. Alternatively, we can descend from Bwlch y Rhiwgyr towards the east, reaching Sylfaen Farm. Follow the narrow public road which winds through Llwynonn before descending to Barmouth.

Chapter 6

ACROSS THE ARANS

Route: Garneddwen – Aran Benllyn – Aran Fawddwy – Dyrysgol -Foel Fawr – Nant Rhos-goch-Garneddwen

Distance: 10 miles

Grade: Strenuous

Starting Point: Pant-Gwyn (Map reference: 851268)

Map: Ordnance Survey "Landranger" (1:50,000) Sheet 124 (Dolgellau and Surrounding Area).

The great and bulky ridge of the Arans has two main summits, the highest is called Aran Fawddwy and rises to 2,970 feet above sea level. It is the highest mountain in Wales outside central Snowdonia, the highest summit of Cadair Idris being 43 feet lower.

Cadair Idris and the Arans are very similar in some ways; the most striking similarity being that they are massifs in the form of great "whale-backs" with a rugged scarp slope on one side, and a steep dip slope on the other. Whereas the summit ridge of Cadair Idris runs from east to west and the mountain exhibits its cliff-girt cwms (hollows) and most dramatic aspect to the north, overlooking the Mawddach estuary, the Arans run as a ridge from north to south and have their dramatic face on the east, overlooking the remote hollows of Cwm Llwyd and Cwm Cowarch.

Because of this particular topography the Arans are not nearly so well known to, or noticed by, the casual visitor to Merionethshire. The massif is best seen, perhaps, from the northern shore of Lake Bala, to the north-east. There the great profile of Aran Benllyn acts as a well balanced background to the wide expanse of the lake, the largest natural sheet of freshwater in Wales.

The east face of Aran Benllyn (2,901 ft) from the head of Cwm Du above Cwm Croes. The agreed right of way crosses the skyline from left to right.

Lake Bala (Llyn Tegid) is a lake of mystery and superstition, of ancient evil and strange happenings though it occupies a wide valley and even in wet weather does not seem, to me, to possess much of the dismal foreboding that tradition bestows on the area. (Tegid was a strong, kind ruler but was finally over-powered and drowned by villains in the lake named in his honour.

Mary Corbett Harris recalls that an old Welsh legend dictates that the Flood started here when an evil monster wallowed out of Llyn Tegid's depths. Upon the summit ridge of the Arans Noah's Ark came to rest as the Flood went down.) Here rises the River Dee, draining the lake at its north-eastern end. However, it might be argued that the Afon Dyfrdwy is the true source of this great river. This mountain stream has its source beneath the eastern cliffs of Dduallt (2,155 feet) and flows into the upper (south-western) end of the lake near the ancient village of Llanuwchllyn.

Another contender for the title of true source of the Dee is the Afon Lliw which drains the remote uplands of Llanuwchllyn parish and rises beneath Moel Llynfant (map reference: 788350).

The east face of Aran Fawddwy (2,970 ft) from Craig Cwm Du

The Route

The main road from Bala to Dolgellau reaches 770 feet above sea level at Pant-gwyn near Garneddwen Halt (map reference: 851268). This is the starting point of the ramble described hereafter.

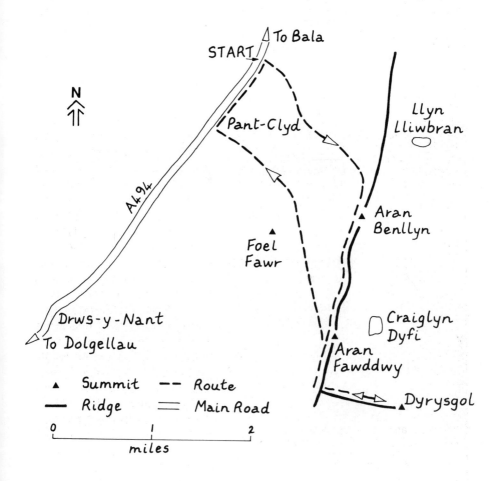

Aran Benllyn – summit views

On my first visit to this spacious Aran summit-ridge the atmosphere was wonderful for long-distance views – very clear but away on every side bright, blue-white fracto-cumulus clouds acted as a wonderful "ceiling" with shafts of sunlight descending and picking out areas of brilliance on many well known, well loved hills of deep blue. The scene reminded me forcibly of a Donegal landscape.

Away towards the sea, Cadair Idris looked surprisingly grassy, the Mawddach gleamed gold between the hazy, noontide slopes and to the west the ancient mountains of the Harlech Dome showed their contrasting profiles to perfection. One of the greatest pleasures of a new summit is the different view of well-known hills and valleys; one gets to know the familiar hills even better by reaching unknown slopes and ridges from which to view them.

The lonely cliffs of Dduallt (map reference: 811274) lie four miles distant "as the crow flies" to the north-west. It is a high ridge dominating part of the wild and lovely land between Bala and Trawsfynydd. Twice as far away, to the right of Dduallt, the beautiful peak of Arenig Fawr hides the lower Arenig Fach and Lake Bala appears to occupy a wide, fertile hollow which has many traditional connections with Arthurian legend.

Far away on the northern horizon on that clear day some of the highest summits of Snowdonia stood blue and solid. Moel Hebog and Snowdon, the Glyders and the Carneddau were easily identifiable beneath that canopy of blue-and-white cloud islands. The top of Snowdon is, incidentally, twenty-four miles distant from Aran Benllyn.

The view over into Cwm Llwyd is surprisingly steep; and green. From the bleached stones forming the cairn the prospect to the east and south-east shows a complete change of country – an area of plateau-moorland dissected by deep troughs, valleys with steep, smooth sides. Looking down into this land of sheepwalk and lonely farms we were able on that sunny day to watch a pair of inky choughs soar in the space below the surprising cliffs that dropped from our perch.

1. For half an hour, make up the steep, regular slopes towards the south-east. In time the top of a level spur is gained at approximately 1,750 feet. Make now for a group of quartz boulders, visible not far ahead as lumps of pure white crystal on the darker slopes. Up steeply now over rocky ground, and in one and three quarter hours (or a little more) we reach the 2,901 feet summit of Aran Benllyn (map reference: 867243).

2. Turn to the south now, along the undulating ridge which in a mile and a half culminates in the 2,970 feet summit of Aran Fawddwy. Looking eastwards from this highest point of the massif one can pick out the Breiddon Hills, far away on the borders of Powys and Shropshire, with the Wrekin behind and the Longmynd (over the border in Shropshire) and Plynlimmon (2,465 feet) nearer us to the south. It is now well worth going on to the south for almost a mile then, turning eastwards, descend the rugged spur called Drws Bach and up to the 2,400 feet conical end of it, called Dyrysgol (map reference; 872213). From here there is an excellent view downwards

into Hengwm at the head of Cwm Cowarch and on in other directions to the "smooth-moor" land of mid-Wales. For me this territory to the south and south-east is not as fascinating, certainly not so exciting, as the true mountains of North Wales.

3. Back now, up the ridge and either over the summit of Aran Fawddwy or by contouring at 2,500 feet gain the westward-flowing headwaters which fall to the Vale of Wnion. In poor visibility it is easy to descend into the wrong torrent-worn valley and so gain the Wnion Valley too low down, involving a longer walk up the road to Pant-gwyn on the watershed.

Avoiding the rocky ground shown on the map at about 2,500 feet overlooking Cwm y Dolau, make over the broad spur called Foel Fawr and so down one of the headstreams which burble down to join the Nant Rhos-goch. Though from this open hillside position the gorge below is invisible, trees soon appear on the steepening flanks and the stream makes some picturesque plunges into rock basins and so leaps on and down into another world.

Before climbing down into this different world of trees and roaring water notice the steep hill-side across the main valley ahead (on the far side of and overlooking the main road and former railway). Through the 1930s my father and mother motored this way towards Barmouth and regularly saw the wild goats which inhabit this high land, rarely seen by the casual visitor. By careful examination of the hillside above the road it was usual to see some goats grazing up there, among the rocks and heather. Sometimes, in the years after the war, we weren't sure whether we were looking at Welsh Mountain sheep or those goats of far-off days.

4. On down into the leafy gorge, close by the plunging water – orange with lichened rocks yet crystal clear in the lovely rock pools. A sheep-worn path leads off to the right and beneath rowans and remarkably large oaks to a smooth, grassy pasture, and here we lay down in the sunshine at the edge of the shade cast by the trees. Over there fly agaric fungi were growing, adding a final touch of magic to our situation.

Far below the torrent was racing, reduced by distance to a whisper. I know of no more idyllic place in my Welsh mountains. A step or two along a level path brings one to this truly "Alpine" pasture, out into the sunshine on the best days of summer when tortoiseshell butterflies dance from one tansy flower to another to the accompaniment of hover flies and the distant Rhos-goch water far below.

5. Finally we got to our feet and sped on down and gained the road after going through Pant-clyd Farm (map reference: 844257). In just less than a mile of walking up the road, towards Bala, we reach Pant-gwyn where this ramble of ten miles began.

Chapter 7

CADAIR IDRIS FROM THE NORTHERN SIDE

An early day on the mountains, geological origin and folklore.

Route A: Barmouth – Arthog – Llynnau Cregennen – Rhiw Gwredydd – Pen-y-Gadair – Tyrau Mawr – Arthog – Barmouth.

Distance: 13 miles

Grade: very strenuous

Starting point: Barmouth (map reference: 618156)

Route B: Llyn Gwernan – Llyn-y-Gafr – Pen-y-Gadair – Mynydd Moel – Lyn Gwernan.

Distance: 5 miles

Grade: strenuous

Starting point: Llyn Gwernan (map reference: 705160)

Maps: Ordnance Survey "Landranger" (1:50,000), Sheet 124 (Dolgellau and Surrounding Area); Ordnance Survey "Outdoor Leisure" (1:25,000), Sheet 23 (Snowdonia – Cadair Idris Area).

Cadair Idris was the first mountain that I climbed, on a hot and sultry day with my father. A day when the visibility was poor, and clouds made our stay on the 2,927 feet summit of Pen-y-Gadair chilly and short. I remember that an old man joined us on the top but he was the only other person we saw that day. Because of that first Welsh mountain day Cadair Idris occupies a special place in my memory of favourite hills.

A glance at the 1:50,000 Ordnance Survey map shows that although the northern face of Cadair Idris presents an almost continuous curtain of cliffs the southern flanks are generally smoother. There are very big cliffs and broken ground on this side but mainly only near the highest summit.

The great northern face of Cadair Idris (2,927 ft) from the hills above the Mawddach at Llwyn-onn

The volcanoes of the Ordovician geological era which poured out the lavas of which most of the mountain is composed must have been on a tremendous scale. Volcanic outpouring with a centre near the present Cadair Idris formed what now constitutes the famous Llyn-y-Gafr group which is largely composed of 1,500 feet of lava flows containing ash and shale bands. The great thicknesses of volcanic rock once covered the older Cambrian rocks of the Harlech Dome hills on the other side of the Mawddach but subsequent erosion has removed all trace of this, and much Cambrian rock too.

Catching the glowing light of the setting sun upon the northern cliff of Cadair Idris from, say, Llwyn-onn or Cutiau or Llyn Gwernan, it is not difficult to imagine the mountain as a volcano, a great, sleeping force of Nature. And mention must here be made of folklore. Idris was a giant who lived here on the mountain, the great hollow beneath the northern cliffs of Pen-y-Gadair with its little lake is said to have been his massive chair – hence, Cadair Idris (the Seat of Idris). But Idris fell from his resting place and slid to the shores of the Mawddach and, looking up the estuary from Barmouth or the Panorama Walk, it is possible to make out the profile of his face and chest on the slope leading up towards the mountain, actually the numerous little hillocks that crown a ridge at about 1,000 feet above sea level between Llyn Gwernan and Penmaen-pool. One summit of this profile used to be marked by a spot height of 1,011 feet on the former 1-inch map, and in the hollow to its east is a small cliff -Craig-y-Castell (the Castle Crag).

In the days before the last war it was "the thing to do" to walk up to the top of Cadair Idris from Barmouth, and most energetic visitors did it regularly. Today this ascent with the relatively long approach is less often done. It is a ramble full of varied interest, starting and ending with the crossing of Barmouth's famous bridge.

One can imagine the protests of those who held the Mawddach's beauty in high regard over a century ago when the Cambrian Railway Company planned to build a viaduct across the mouth of the estuary. What is more the coming of a railway would undermine much of Barmouth's importance as a seaport where many fine timber vessels were built. The line built from Bala, over the 770 foot pass at the head of the Wnion Valley and down to Dolgellau was then to skirt the southern shore of the Mawddach to meet the coastal line coming up from Towyn in the south at Barmouth Junction. The single track would then cross the estuary and pass through Barmouth *en route* for Harlech, Criccieth and Pwllheli. A line down the side of the Mawddach and a viaduct across its beautiful mouth! Hands were held up in horror, but, nevertheless, the railway company proceeded with their plans and in 1866 the Barmouth Bridge was built, with its swing section at the northern (Barmouth) end to allow tall vessels to pass upstream.

Though there were voices raised in protest it is likely that the outcry was far less than it would be today, when more people appreciate beautiful countryside and are prepared to do something to conserve it as it is reduced annually by the greedy and the thoughtless. Over a century ago the seafarers and shipbuilders of the Mawddach suffered most, for the railway soon proved an easier and speedier means of transporting coal, provisions and people.

Route "A"

1. There is no road bridge across the Mawddach until one reaches Penmaenpool seven miles upstream from the sea, and that is private and a toll must be paid. There is, however, a footpath across the Barmouth Bridge and it provides 751 yards of fresh, sea air and downward glimpses of the moving waters or wet sand crossed by searching oyster catchers which bleep from salty pool to salty pool left by the tide between the solid sable ripples.

2. As we cross the bridge towards Cadair Idris notice Ynys y Brawd (Monk's isle) lying in the mouth of the estuary. This constituted both a useful shelter for the harbour and a hazard for vessels when Barmouth was a busy seaport. Attempts to light the island for visiting ships were singularly unsuccessful – in 1839 a four-sided stone tower was built to a height of twenty feet above high water mark before a storm demolished it. In 1843 a new lighthouse was erected to fifteen feet, only to be swept away by another angry sea. Today a beacon on a pole lights the masonry breakwater at the corner of Ynys y Brawd.

> **Barmouth Lifeboat**
>
> Just before reaching the gate at the northern end of the bridge, (where a toll must be paid) notice the roof of the Barmouth Lifeboat Station. The slipway lies beneath the footpath and railway track, directing the lifeboat out into deep water above the harbour. Mr William Morris was for a long time the first mechanic of this lifeboat, and in 1958 received the Maud Smith Award for the bravest act of life-saving by a member of a lifeboat crew in 1957. On July 16th, 1957 a number of bathers got into difficulties on Barmouth's beach and William Morris put out in his motor launch with the winchman of the Barmouth Lifeboat, George Berridge. In order to save time they took the boat through a narrow, sandy channel where she touched bottom several times, but by skilful handling Morris got through to the open sea, which was becoming increasingly rough. There they managed to save three girls and a boy who were exhausted and fast being carried out by the ebb tide.

3. As one leaves the southern end of the bridge there is a path forking left towards the hillock called Fegla Fawr (once an island in the estuary before deposition of silt and sand turned this coast into level salt marsh) and this path will take one directly over the drained marsh to Arthog village. Otherwise, continue alongside the railway line to Barmouth Junction, and so by the main road to Arthog, a longer and less pleasant route.

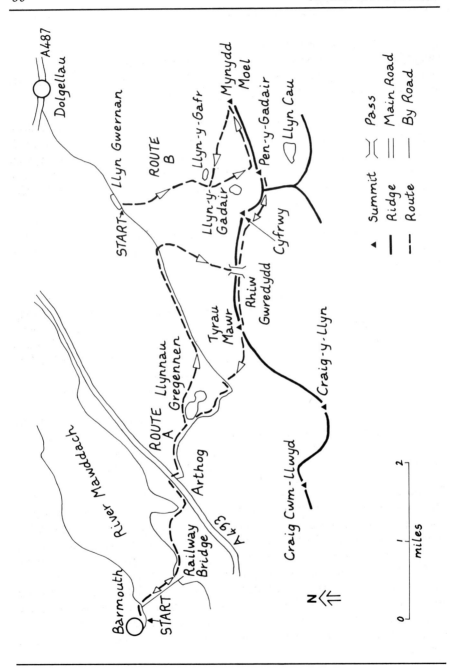

4. For the next couple of miles it may be better to have a copy of the Ordnance Survey "Outdoor leisure" (1:25,000) Sheet 23 (Cadair Idris Area) as the paths and tracks leading up the slopes from Arthog towards Cadair Idris are many and can be most misleading.

5. Where the main road crosses the Afon Arthog (often called Arthog Waterfalls) there is a church (map reference: 646146). Just beyond a track climbs up and soon crosses the Afon Arthog, then turns to cross it again. A track continues up a side-valley which is wooded and eventually comes to Gefnir Isaf Farm (map reference: 657148) where we double-back towards the twin lakes of Llynnau Cregennen. The path skirts this lovely hollow on the northern shore of the larger lake. Over the ridge ahead and down into a sheltered valley we soon reach Nant-y-gwyrddail Farm and so along the track to the tarmac lane leading towards Llyn Gwernan and Dolgellau for about one mile.

6. Just before a lane turns down to the left, to the old chapel at Ty'n-y-ceunant, a path leads up the slope towards Cadair idris (map reference: 690149). The path zig-zags upwards for six hundred feet, where it joins another path which slants up to this level from Ty-nant Farm. In clear weather the Saddle (the 1,838 foot pass of Rhiw Gwredydd between Cadair Idris proper and its westward continuation as Tyrau Mawr) is clearly visible to the south less than a mile away.

7. In poor visibility the path can be followed with confidence as it climbs ever more steeply for almost seven hundred feet. Once upon the Saddle or pass or col or, more correctly here, the Bwlch face to the east and commence the gentle walk over sparse grasses and bare stone.

8. The track by-passes the summit of the secondary top, called Cyfrwy. This has a black and splintered northern face looking down upon Llyn y Gadair, but unseen from this side until the path suddenly comes to the crest of a steep face dropping to the north. Very soon the ground drops away on the southern side too. The ridge ahead seems to be narrowing and driving us onto something approaching a tight-rope! On my first visit mists were curling in and obscured the great drop to the north and the space of a black hollow to the south, above which rose the small, stony summit above Craig Lwyd. The topography seemed incomprehensible – that far top appeared completely unattainable in the swirling vapour.

9. Very soon one is standing at the triangulation station on the 2,927 feet summit of Pen-y-Gadair, the top of Cadair Idris. Here one can look in all directions into the great, ice-worn cwms and along weathered ridges and wonder at the vastness of the range on its apparent progress from land to the western sea.

10. Return now towards the east, down to Rhiw Gwredydd and up to the 2,167 feet top of the narrow ridge which presents a steep, broken face to the Mawddach and is so well seen from above Barmouth and Cutiau. It is called Tyrau Mawr but the broken, northern face is Craig-las. The distance is approximately three miles from Pen-y-Gadair.

On the Summit

Down to the north little Llyn y Gadair lies below the sombre shadow of Cyfrwy and behind, in the great hollow called "The Devil's Punchbowl" or Cwm Cau, lies Lyn Cau. This little pool always has a sombre look, a dismal dullness cast by the encircling cliffs where ravens croak their wicked chants from ledge to ledge above the shadowed void. Here came that great landscape artist, Richard Wilson, to paint "Llyn-y-Cau, Cadair Idris" which became known as "Wilson's Pool". Born near Machynlleth in 1714 Richard Wilson became, to quote Geoffrey Grigson, "the first great interpreter of the illuminated skies, the blue mountains and valleys of Wales".

Just below the summit of Pen-y-Gadair, to the east, is a rough shed of stone. Here cups of tea were once served. The caterer professed to bring the water up here daily in a barrel slung upon the back of a donkey. A party my father was with one pre-war summer's day filled up their tea-cups with hot water from the kettle on the fire and were immediately charged another shilling each! The water was indeed precious. It was strange, however, that the lady caterer had not discovered the spring of clear water not many yards away above the top of the Fox's Path! And where was that donkey? It was never seen on the summit.

An old man called Brown living in Dolgellau claimed not many years ago to have climbed the mountain once a day for five days a week for many years. I forget the exact number of ascents that he made, but it certainly ran into many hundreds. He, like so many mountain lovers, never tired of a particular piece of high ground, finding details to interest him on every ascent.

11. We now drop increasingly steeply towards the lane at Hafotty-fach Farm (map reference: 660134) being careful to avoid the broken ground beneath the western cliffs of Craig-las.

12. Numerous lanes now wind down to Arthog but if time allows choose the one which goes down by Pant-y-llan Farm, and just below are the ruins of ancient Llys Bradwen, a great house of considerable importance but now reduced to a few grassy mounds by the Afon Arthog (map reference: 650139). In less than a mile of downhill going we reach Arthog and turn left along the road, turning right along

the lane to Barmouth Junction, and so by the railway and over the bridge to Barmouth, so completing a mountain day of about thirteen miles which would normally take most of a summer day.

Route "B"

The quickest way to the highest summit of Cadair Idris is by the well-trodden Fox's Path from Lyn Gwernan.

1. A narrow lane leads south-westwards from Dolgellau, the old route above the Mawddach *en route* to Towyn and Aberdovey. Two miles from the town the lane skirts the southern shore of lovely Llyn Gwernan (map reference: 705160). Here stands the Gwernan Lake Hotel and among the bamboo skirting the lake's fringe waterfowl swim. The path leaves the lane at 573 feet above sea level opposite the hotel and climbs steep grass and bracken-slopes; in a mile traversing marshy ground.

2. As we come into sight of Llyn y Gafr resting in its smooth hollow there is a good view to the great frontal precipices of the eastern summit, called Mynydd Moel (2,804 feet). Above the steeper slope ahead the dark pinnacles of Cyfrwy threaten and the highest summit of Pen-y-Gadair stands solidly behind. After breasting this steep slope the cliff-surrounded lake called Llyn y Gadair is reached, passing a spot height of 1,837 feet. This lake often possesses a glassy surface and never assumes the sinister character of many pools contained within the glacier-worn hollows of North Wales.

The northern cliffs of Cadair Idris are notoriously loose and have, since the birth of serious British mountaineering, deterred much exploration of their less accessible slabs and buttresses. A number of climbers have been killed or injured on these cliffs, and Owen Glynne Jones had some breathtaking moments when making the first ascent of Cyfrwy's Arete alone in 1888.

3. Directly above us the red screes and rutted track of the Fox's Path leads to the left of the summit of Pen-y-Gadair. We have about 1,100 feet to climb now and the steep section of about 1,000 feet will not take so long as might be expected. I have gone up this section in eighteen minutes without pressing the pace.

4. On reaching the broad summit turn to the right (west) and very soon the 2,927 foot top is gained. From Llyn Gwernan to this summit will take $1^1/_2$ hours of quick progress without a long stop, but 2 hours or more if details of the views and terrain hereabouts are to be savoured.

In clear weather the slate quarrying village of Upper Corris is visible 3.5 miles to the south-east in the valley leading to the Afon Dulas and Machynlleth. To the north the summit of Y Wyddfa, highest point of the Snowdon massif, partly hides 27 miles distant behind the remote and rugged Y Garn (2,063 feet) and the lonely tops of the Rhinogs.

5. Our route now lies to the east, across the wide, smooth ridge to Mynydd Moel. This walk will take approximately 25 minutes. From this high hill-end one can look down on three steep, rocky sides – towards Talyllyn, over the broken ground Dolgellau-wards and to the golden sands of Mawddach with the dark heights of the Harlech Dome behind, a whole world to be trodden in a dozen lifetimes without complete discovery.

6. Down now towards the west, making for Llyn y Gafr. The steep ground soon eases and we traverse boulder-strewn slopes. It is not necessary to go right down to the little lake's shore, instead keep over to the right and go down by the main stream of this wide hollow. Soon we join the lower section of the Fox's path and so back to the lane by Llyn Gwernan. One can make the descent from the summit of Mynydd Moel to Llyn Gwernan in one hour, though a longer time is needed in misty conditions or in snow and ice.

Cadair Idris is a popular mountain and I have never visited its summit when it has been entirely deserted. On many summer days literally hundreds of ramblers visit the summits, but if solitude is required go there in spring or late autumn, when the views are often clearer and the colouring brighter than in late summer.

Chapter 8

HILLS OF THE HARLECH DOME

Route A: Cwm Nantcol – Rhinog Fawr – Bwlch Drws Ardudwy -Rhinog Fach – Y Llethr – Moelfre – Cwm Nantcol.

Distance: 8.5 miles

Grade: Strenuous

Starting Point: Cwm Nantcol (map reference: 642269)

Route B: As above to Y Llethr – Crib-y-rhiw – Diffwys -Llawlech – Barmouth

Distance: 12 miles.

Grade: Very Strenuous

Starting Point: Cwm Nantcol (map reference: 642269)

Route C: Cwm Bychan – Roman Steps – Bwlch Tyddiad – Rhinog Fawr – Bwlch Tyddiad – Craig Wion – Clip – Cwm Bychan

Distance: 6.5 miles.

Grade: Strenuous.

Starting Point: Cwm Bychan (map reference: 648315)

Maps: Ordnance Survey "Landranger" (1:50,000) Sheet 124, (Dolgellau and Surrounding Area); Ordnance Survey "Outdoor Leisure" (1:25,000), Sheet 18 (Snowdonia – Harlech and Bala Area).

In the great roadless country between the Mawddach estuary and the Vale of Ffestiniog and between the sea-coast and the valley of the Afon Eden rises a toppled mass of ancient mountains unlike any others in Britain.

They are composed of Cambrian rocks, the largest surface exposure of such rocks in the British Isles. Their summits once rose to many thousands of feet above the sea, much higher than the now-higher tops of Cadair Idris to the south and central Snowdonia to the north. These upper areas have slowly been denuded, eroded by the constant action of frost, wind, sun and ice, and such erosion is still taking place so that one day these wonderful hills and their valley-cradled lakes will vanish from the earth's surface.

Winter sunlight on Moelfre (1,932 ft) to the left and the Llawlech ridge from near Llanfair, Harlech.

Route "A"

1. The first ramble starts in lonely Cwm Nantcol, where the narrow lane leading up from Llanbedr ends at Maes-y-Garnedd Farm (map reference: 642269). Here is quite a wide cwm with the dark bulk of the Rhinogs ahead to the east, separated by the dramatic pass leading towards Trawsfynydd and Afon Eden, called Bwlch Drws Ardudwy. Rhinog Fach (right) appears the more dramatic peak of the pair from here.

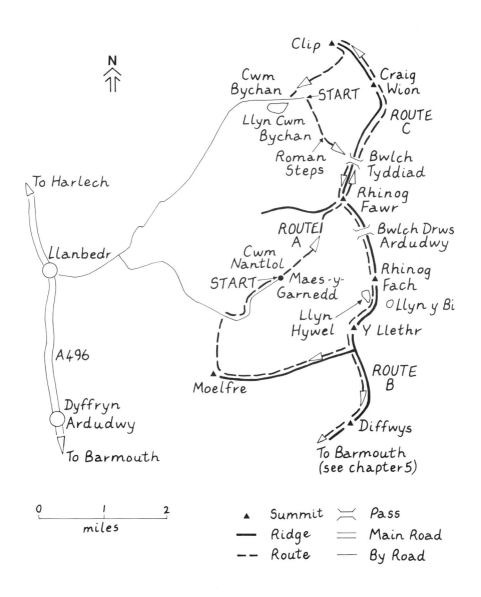

2. Make now for Rhinog Fawr, the left-hand peak above the deep pass ahead, and the highest of the twin mountains. Be prepared for difficult going for it has been stated by more than one authority (and I agree) that the Rhinogs present the most broken mountainous ground south of the Scottish Highlands. Great masses of tumbled boulders lie half-hidden amongst the heather and bracken, much is loose and care must be taken.

3. One can either follow the path straight up to the top of the pass (map reference: 665282) and then turn up to the north, ascending 1,200 feet up the mountain's south ridge to the triangulation station on the 2,362 foot summit, or make a slower, but more direct, route from the place where the pass narrows to a defile (map reference: 652277.)

The Civil War

Maes-y-Garnedd Farm is a typical, low-built structure of great antiquity. Here was born in the early years of the seventeenth century John Jones. For some unexplained reason he went to London when a young man as an apprentice, later to join the household of the Lord Mayor of London, Sir Thomas Middleton. In 1642 the Civil War broke out and Jones joined the Parliamentary forces. Because of outstanding valour he was soon made a Captain of Infantry and thereafter became a Member of Parliament. Not long afterwards, through the influence of Cromwell, he was created a Knight of the Shire of Merionethshire in 1647. By this time John Jones had become a Colonel and henceforward he became "an instrument in all Cromwell's plots and treasons against the King".

Ultimately Colonel Jones became a Commissioner of Parliament for the Government of Ireland, an office he is said to have "discharged with great tyranny" as he followed his strict rules of Puritanism against "the laxity of the Irish". In 1648 Colonel Jones was given one thousand pounds by Parliament for his great services. So important had he become that he was called upon in January 1649 to sign the death warrant of King Charles I. Later he returned from Ireland and married Cromwell's sister. Colonel Jones had three sons, but whether by this wife or his former wife, Margaret Stansty, is not known.

Following Oliver Cromwell's death Jones plotted against the Government under the control of Cromwell's son, Richard, but after the Restoration he came in for the full fury of the Cavalier Parliament. Evelyn records that on October 17th, 1660, Jones and three other regicides – Scott, Cook and Scrope – "suffered for reward of their iniquities at Charing Crosse, in the sight of the place where they put to death their natural Prince ...".

So this son of the high hills rose in importance in the land, but, in the end suffered his well-earned punishment, and today we look back upon him as an evil-doer. The lonely hills bred, and still breed, men or rare genius, often artists or poets, more rarely men with the soldiering qualities of John Jones. It is interesting to note that until recent years members of his family continued to inhabit Maes-y-Garnedd.

If the latter way is taken, tend to keep over to the west and so get up onto the south-western flank, which is smoother, easier. From the road-head to the summit via Bwlch Drws Ardudwy should take about one hour and twenty minutes.

Summit Views

In clear conditions the views from the summit of Rhinog Fawr are wonderful. To the north-west a glimpse of Llyn Cwm Bychan is had, beyond the rugged slopes of Carreg-y-saeth. Down there, in that sombre hollow of shade and echoes, is a land of eerie "presence" – a place of unusual atmosphere in which I have never been really happy. What is it, this feeling of eyes-upon-one that pervades Cwm Bychan?

Eastwards and south-eastwards the view from the top is of wide moorland and extensive coniferous forest. A great proportion of the land flanking the headwaters of the Mawddach and its right-bank tributary, the Afon Eden, has been used by the Forestry Commission in the last half-century, so that today thousands of acres are dark and secret from within but fresh and verdant from without, as the spruces, pines and firs grow towards maturity. From Rhinog Fawr this is an eastern world of level bog, heather and a million green tree-tops.

Away to the west-north-west Criccieth, nearest of the Lleyn resorts, is about 11 miles distant and beyond the land of Lleyn looks happy with little hills and sunny strands and sparkling seas. To the south we look along the backbone of the Harlech Dome to the other summits – Rhinog Fach, Y Llethr and Diffwys, with the broad breast of Moelfre standing along towards the sea. This is the land which we are going now to explore, a high ridge-land with the almost forgotten kingdom of Ardudwy between us and the shores of Cardigan Bay to the west.

4. If a direct descent to the road-head at Nantcol is required it will take about three-quarters of an hour from this highest top.

5. Our route now lies to the south, directly down to the top of the pass -Bwlch Drws Ardudwy – and then up the steep northern ridge of Rhinog Fach. The ascent is approximately 1,150 feet and may take as much as one hour on account of the typically rugged nature of the ridge.

Rhinog Fach (2,333 feet) is the better looking mountain of the pair, presenting a bold, if truncated, profile to both east and west. Though 29 feet lower than its bigger neighbour it looks the higher from most viewpoints. Away to the south is lovely Y Llethr, lovely yet enigmatic – a peak of mystery and other-worldliness, other-worldliness in the sense that many imagined or yearned-for things of childhood and youth take on an unreal quality. A dark yet fresh-green mountain, a forbidding yet welcoming mountain.

6. Y Llethr (2,475 feet) is the highest point of the Harlech Dome, and to reach it from Rhinog Fach we must descend to the narrow col between deep Llyn Hywel, home of horrific,

one-eyed fish which rarely swim near surface or shore, and little Llyn y Bi on the eastern flanks of the Dome – a stretch of water marking the central point of a comparatively large area of National Trust property. The col is just over 1,750 feet above sea level, over-shadowed by Y Llethr's narrow north ridge which rises for 700 feet to the summit. In misty conditions remember to keep to the south-west, otherwise one will miss the ridge and go down the steep slope towards the south-east, so missing the mountain altogether.

Winter in Cwm Nantcol, looking to Bwlch Drws Ardudwy, Rhinog Fawr (centre) and Rhinog Fach(right)

I always get a thrill on gaining the top of the mountain and will never forget the wonderful feeling of the earth falling away as we got to the summit one summer's afternoon in 1965. A few Welsh Mountain ewes grazed the sun-soaked sword on the rounded top, white fracto-cumulus clouds dotted the blue sky, archipelago-like. Away to the north and north-west the mountains of Snowdonia and Lleyn stood clear like a dark blue frieze. The wind blew fresh from the sea – what a contrast with that day long ago, recorded by Winthrop Young in such a way as to be one of the most beautiful sentences in mountain literature, when grey cloud clothed this many-walled mountain -walls still there, like the sheep and the view to Lleyn.

7. Now for the long run down the ridge called Moelyblithcwm, an easy, grassy slope of almost two miles to the west. Then up the broad breast of Moelfre. This is a real conical mountain, a pap or rounded breast, full-dome if any hill was. In days of grey and lowering cloud Moelfre wears a cap, and in certain conditions takes on the appearance of a gigantic mountain, a Kilimanjaro or Etna. Yet in reality Moelfre is only 1,932 feet high. It is a hill of history; upon the summit is an ancient cairn, probably built by the mysterious people who lived in the wild and level basin of Ardudwy which it dominates. From its summit, too, tradition states that King Arthur hurled a large stone (a quoit) to the valley floor. That old quoit can still be seen in the lowland below Moelfre.

Three and a half miles away to the west-north-west lies the northern tip of the extensive sand-dune complex called Morfa Dyffryn which long-shore drift in Cardigan Bay has piled up and so isolated the settlements of Tal-y-Bont, Dyffryn and Llanbedr from the sea. Behind the extensive sandhills is a low and marshy tract of alluvial land which widens to the north, culminating in the sandy mouth of the Afon Artro.

Wild Goats

Upon the Rhinogs roam wild goats – truly wild they are. It is stated that these are the last authentic wild goats in Wales, and I believe they are, for this is the most likely place of all for them to live, safe from many human intrusions. The goats normally live together in one or more groups, splitting up when danger or poor feeding conditions require it. One notable authority stated recently that only one glimpse of the herd has been recorded in the last half-century, but I cannot uphold this as I have occasionally come upon them in secret corners of the rocks.

In the summer of 1965, upon a warm day of heavy, though high, cloud, we ascended the rough terrain to the south-west of the summit of Rhinog Fawr and smelt the pungent odour of the goats. Topping a steep slope of boulders and stiff heather we were able to look across to the browsing animals, a group of seven I recall. One must, of course, be down-wind of them to observe them for any time. If they once see, hear or "feel" one's presence they will make off and melt into the fastness of rocks. During the winter the goats wander as far as the slopes above Llwyn-onn, overlooking the Mawddach's northern shore.

Mochras

Upon certain parts of the beach at Mochras are to be found a large quantity of sea shells of molluscs and crustaceans and because of this the place has become known over the decades as "Shell Island". There is a solitary farm upon Mochras where the remarkable poet Sion Philip lived in the early part of the seventeenth century. The effects of isolation caused by the moods of the sea or the mountains upon an imaginative mind have probably been responsible for much of the poetry and bardic writing which has come out of the wild mountains of Wales, so that perhaps Sion Philip is not so remarkable a character after all – many of the greatest imaginative creations of man have been engendered by closeness to the natural world, hence the affinity of Welsh mountains and the poetic spirit of simple and intelligent people.

While isolated upon Mochras in 1620 by a great storm Philip created his most famous poem "Cywydd" – "Ode to the Seagull". Listen to this powerful writing about the things around him, and imagine it in the infinitely more expressive and beautiful language in which it was written:

O thou fair seagull on the water's edge
With thy bosom of shining feathers, and
of strong condition,
No huntsman shall capture thee nor
pursue thee,
Water shall drown thee not, nor shall
any man possess thee,
Though art a nun whose nourishment is
a mouthful from the sea ...

And further on the poet brings the dark mountains of the Harlech Dome which formed an eastern wall or background for him into the complexity of the tempestuous sea surrounding him on his island as he waited and wrote:

The cruel wind has winnowed the
gravel,
Has rendered bare the crags which are
the home of the whirlwind,
Inky has been the colour of the stormy
whirlpool
Where the western wind is blowing ...

Partly blocking the mouth of this little creek is the "island" of Mochras, really an old islet reaching over 50 feet above sea level but now solidly joined to the coast by sand-dunes.

8. To do justice to this rushy land of curlew's calls and broken clouds one would need a complete chapter devoted to the antiquities alone, but let the foregoing be an appetite-whetter. So from the top of Moelfre we turn to the north and descend for a mile and 1,300 feet to the road junction (map reference: 626259), then turn eastwards to the starting point at Nantcol or westwards, down to the coast.

Route "B"

As an alternative finish to the above route one can continue upon the high backbone of the Dome from Y Llethr's top, southwards for 8.5 miles to Barmouth or Bontddu.

1. Descend southwards on to the relatively level and narrow ridge connecting Y Llethr and Diffwys called Crib-y-rhiw. This is a very pleasant place in fine weather, grass and rocks mingling and there are extensive and interest-

ing views. Cardigan Bay is seen to advantage, and so is the Lleyn peninsula, with Bardsey Island standing clear of the promontory's tip from this angle. To the north-east the white cubes of the nuclear power station on the shores of Trawsfynydd Lake are distinct seven miles away.

On the way the northern face of Diffwys is seen to exhibit the clearly curved strata of a downfold, or syncline, which has been much eroded. The rocks forming the summit area of this hill are Barmouth Grits, middle-aged rocks of the Cambrian era. Surrounding these grits to the north and east is an exposure of older Manganese Shales. In fact there are the remains of a manganese mine high up on the eastern flanks of Diffwys, where the shales were once exploited for their rich manganese content.

As we go towards Diffwys, the lake called Bodlyn is visible below to the west, at 1,250 feet above sea level at the head of the great hollow already referred to. In 1890 Llyn Bodlyn started to be used as the main source of water supply for Barmouth, its depth being increased by a masonry dam to create a capacity of 102 million gallons. The lake today covers 40 acres, and the collecting area is about 900 acres. Because the average annual rainfall hereabouts is in excess of 80 inches Llyn Bodlyn has proved a sufficient reservoir for the town.

On the dark and miserable cliffs overlooking the lake's southern shore is a tablet to the memory of a young man killed here while bird nesting many years ago. It suggests for me the sombre nature of this hollow.

Higher up and nearer our route is the smaller lake called Llyn Dulyn. A wildly sited pool which can be easily missed, so closely surrounded by rocks and steep slopes to the east and north. This is the lake which was once "noted for a race of trout which have most peculiar heads". It is possible that Giraldus Cambrensis heard of this tradition and so recorded them as being "the monstrous species" in the twelfth century.

2. The walk from Y Llethr to the top of Diffwys takes about one hour. From this wonderful viewpoint we look across the huge spaces of the hollow occupied by the estuary of the Mawddach to the great, eroded northern precipices of Ordovician rock on Cadair Idris.

Antiquities

Back upon Moelfre's rounded summit on a fine day we look down to the broad hollow on the south side which is drained by the Afon Ysgethin. Here the land of Llanddwywe-is-y-Craig, a land of great antiquity and a seat of heathendom, looks out from its elevated levels to the coast of Cardigan Bay and the level line of the western horizon.

Days of interest can be had in this area, exploring the cromlechau and carneddau which litter a region once quite densely populated but now without inhabitants, save for the curlew and the buzzard, the crow, the heron and others like wandering herring gulls in from the sea.

Looking at the western flanks of the Harlech Dome on an Ordnance Survey map reveals the many antiquities lying there – actually there are far more than the ones shown on the 1:50,000 map, scores of almost imperceptible mounds colonised now by bracken and moss and reed-beds.

Upon the 1,164 feet high mound called Craig-y-Dinas (map reference: 624230) is the ruin of a Druidical circle – a wall with an oblique entrance and two stone ramparts are all that remain. Here the rites of these priests of the Gods of the Goidels and the Brythons were performed, here they had their heathen temples. The stones we look at or sit upon on these brown hill-slopes may have been the Maen Llog (the Stone of the Covenant) upon which was placed a sheathed sword at the commencement of each ceremony.

At 860 feet above sea level (map reference: 613205) are the huge remnants of the Carneddau Hengwm – burial mounds of important druids. Over a mile to the north-east is the dark, oval lake called Llyn Irddyn and not far from this silent place renowned for char are more remains; two are chomlechau – Cist Faen and Maen Hir – which are rectangular in form. Nearby, to the east, is a large altar built of two sloping stones.

3. If we are descending to Bontddu take the steep and broken route to the south, down over Craig Aderyn and so into the cwm of Hirgwm, gaining a track at the farm of Hafod-uchaf (map reference: 659211). Now down a lovely valley for two miles to the village above the estuary's shore.

4. Alternatively we proceed south-westwards from the summit, towards Barmouth. Keep to the broad, level ridge to the west which becomes Llawlech and rises to 1,930 feet above the wide hollow where stand the ancient Sword Stones and the now derelict Golodd. By the way, the ascent from Llwyn-onn (map reference: 628178) via Golodd to the top of Diffwys takes $2^1/_2$ hours. Crossing our descending ridge is the ancient trackway once the main link between Dolgellau and Harlech and known as the "Old Harlech Track". The route winds up the south-facing ridge from Bontddu, crosses Llawlech at 1,830 feet and so winds down the steeper flank to cross the Afon Ysgethin at Pont Scethin (map reference: 634235) and so on towards the coast near Llanbedr.

At the point where the track turns sharply down to Pont

Scethin is a grave-like slab of slate to the memory of the remarkable lady referred to in chapter 5.

It may be worth mentioning here that a relatively quick route can be made from the top of Y Llethr to Llwyn-onn, via Pont Scethin and this track, taking about $2^1/_2$ hours.

5. Proceeding over Llawlech we drop to the next pass in the ridge, the famous Bwlch y Rhiwgyr. Here a broad path also crosses from Llanbedr southwards to the Mawddach's shores at Cutiau. It is actually possible to ride a motorcycle over this lonely pass with care and some skill, though parts are relatively marshy. As in many places on this broad ridge the lovely Stagshorn Clubmoss grows in abundance, sending up its yellow-scaled cones on long stalks.

6. Descend, now, towards the south-west and gain the track leading from Llwyn-onn to Golodd at a point close to where a stream goes under it (map reference: 633194), and so along by Sylfaen Farm and Llwyn-onn and, two miles further down, to Barmouth.

Route "C"

The final ramble which I have room to describe here is towards the northern side of the Harlech Dome. The lovely Afon Artro has its source in the dark and sinister waters of Llyn Cwm Bychan, a small and well known lake whose surface stands just over 500 feet above sea level and frowned upon by the usual toppled crags of this area. The lake is fed by a number of torrents, the largest draining the western slopes of Craig Wion to the east of Cwm Bychan.

The lane up to Cwm Bychan leaves the centre of Llanbedr and in about five miles the lake is reached where, according to a lesser Victorian poet,

The ripple washing in the reeds
And the wild water lapping on the crag.

All around are sombre steeps of grey, or in cloudy conditions, black, and Cwm Bychan possesses, for me at least, an evil spirit or a restless atmosphere, a region of indefinable ill-grace.

Here was made that great Indian-set film *The Drum*, and here Sabu rode his elephant and guns roared from a simulated frontier-land among the toppled crags above.

Here, too, is one of the best placed I know for hearing an echo. As one walks eastwards along the lane above the lake a large cliff on the opposite shore is drawn abreast of. It is upon this rock that sounds can be made to rebound; the best place is from the lane not far along the lake-side from the Artro's outflow.

Herons may be seen striding in the reed-beds here, whilst crows and an occasional raven fly from crag to crag beneath an often grey sky. In spring wrens may be sighted by the lane and lake-side.

Less than one-third of a mile beyond the lake's upper end stands the ancient farm of Cwm Bychan. When Pennant came here in 1779 Ieunan Llwyd was in residence. This man claimed lineal descent from the "lords who had dwelt secure among those mountains since at least the year 1100". These were the descendants of Cadwgan, arch-protagonists against the son of Uchtryd ab Edwyn. For centuries the feud continued, fight after fight for control of land and grazing animals. Finally the Cadwgan family were victorious, exterminating their enemies.

Pennant records that Ieunan Llwyd was living in an atmosphere of medieval simplicity when he visited him. He explained to the former that upon the departure of one of his esteemed ancestors to do battle with Risiart Fradwr (Richard III) the song "Ffarwel Dai Llwyd", a farewell to the lord of this wild territory, was composed. He also showed Pennant the ancient family cup, fashioned from the skin of a bull's scrotum, and the remarkable Cistie Styssylog which were great chests (presumably of native oak) used for the winter storage of oatmeal.

Ieunan Llwyd was an enterprising landowner and one of his more exotic schemes consisted of an attempt to drain Cwm Bychan Lake to add to the acreage of level land and so grow more oats, and produce more hay for winter feeding. This plan, of course, never came to fruition, and the lake remains today in much the same state as two centuries ago.

1. Beyond the old farm the road ends (map reference: 648315) and a track swings southwards, climbing gradually through scattered native woodland. We follow this for one and a half miles to the summit of the pass of 1,450 feet called Bwlch Tyddiad. The ascent of over 900 feet is through trees, then open slopes and later through broken rocks and small crags. The route is well marked and soon we are treading on a substantial causeway of paving stones, there are flights of steps between the heather. This is the world-renowned Roman Steps on the route from Llanbedr and the Cardigan Bay coast over the Harlech Dome eastwards to the upper valley of the Afon Eden in the vicinity of Trawsfynydd.

Tradition has it that this is a Roman route, laid with slabs and steps to enable troops to travel easily between their notable fort of Tomen-y-Mûr on Sarn Helen (map reference: 706387) and the coast. If the Romans had desired such a route they would surely have used the lower and more direct pass of Bwlch Drws Ardudwy to the south. It seems likely that the so-called Roman Steps were built in medieval times to facilitate trade between east and west, especially the transport of animals and farm produce by pack animals.

Just beyond the top of the pass, a little way down on the eastward slope, is a well which can be most welcome on a hot, dry summer's day. It is marked on the Ordnance Survey map.

2. From the top of the pass ascend to the south for a mile to the rocky summit of Rhinog Fawr, passing the lovely little pool of Llyn Du (the Black Lake). Descend again to the pass the way one has come and proceed now northwards, climbing to the first little summit of 1,701 feet and on over the very broken ground. In cloudy weather it is best to keep to the very top of this broad and craggy ridge, in a mile gaining the top of the next hill called Craig Wion at 1,850 feet above sea level. Actually there are two long and narrow summits here, the eastern one being a little more than 60 feet lower. Between the two is little Llyn Pryfed.

3. Dropping down to the north again another pool is passed and beyond it are the fascinating remains of a hut circle dating from pre-historic times (map reference: 664325). Proceeding to the north-west over more broken ground the 1,937 feet high top of Clip is reached after crossing the path which crosses here from Cwm Bychan to Trawsfynydd Lake and village beneath the dark rocks of Craig Ddrwg.

4. It is now a simple matter to descend to this path again and so down to Cwm Bychan, about 1.5 miles from Clip's top, to complete this route of 6.5 miles.

Alternatively, it makes a grand, though much longer day, to continue upon the main watershed of the Harlech Dome from the summit of Clip. After Craig Ddrwg comes the highest hill-top north of Rhinog Fawr – the lonely mass called Moel Ysgyfarnogod (2,046 feet) overlooking a forlorn land of scattered pools and ancient trackways. Down to the north-west are the standing stones of Bryn Cader-faner and the cairn circles by the track leading towards Llandecwyn.

Continuing northwards from this high hill rough ground is traversed for almost three miles, eventually reaching the track near Llyn Llennyrch and so by Tallin the way leads either northwards down through woods to Maentwrog in the Vale of Ffestiniog or westwards down to Llandecwyn and so to the main road at Talsarnau.

Pont Fadog, over the Afon Ysgethin near Cors-y-Gedol

Chapter 9

ARENIG FAWR AND ARENIG FACH

Route: Pont Rhyd-y-fen – Arenig Fawr – Llyn Arenig Fawr – Pont Rhyd-y-fen – Y Foel – Arenig Fach – Llyn Arenig Fach.

Distance: 10 miles

Grade: Moderate

Starting Point: Pont Rhyd-y-fen (map reference: 820394)

Maps: Ordnance Survey "Landranger" (1:50,000) Sheet 124 (Dolgellau and Surrounding Area); Ordnance Survey "Outdoor Leisure" (1:25,000) Sheet 18 (Snowdonia – Harlech and Bala Area).

There exists a great area of upland in North Wales which could be said to be almost unknown to most ramblers and mountaineers. It is that vast region lying to the north of the Bala-Dolgellau trough, to the east of the Eden-Trawsfynydd-Ffestiniog trough and to the south of Lledr-upper Conwy trough. There are many fine hills, many rarely trodden, including remote Rhobell Fawr (2,408 feet) and Dduallt (2,155 feet) in the south, Moel Llyfnant (2,461 feet) and the Arenigs in the centre and Manod Mawr (2,166 feet), Ro-wen (1,961 feet) and Carnedd-y-Filiast (2,194 feet) in the north.

The highest mountain in all this wild and lonely region is that of Arenig Fawr (2,800 feet). Few British summits attain an easily-remembered "round" figure, but this mountain is an exception.

Seen from the south, from a good distance away near Bala Lake, Arenig Fawr (or the Big Arenig to be correct) looks a fine, a beautiful mountain. Its conical summit balances gracefully the bulky, off-centre shoulders and the rugged ground which extends in front between Carreg y Diocyn and Craig y Bychan. In certain lights the mountain looks rose-pink and most welcoming from this southerly viewpoint, beckoning to one to walk over the intervening upland by the Roman fort called Caer Gai (map reference: 878314) and the ancient cairn beneath Moel Ymenyn to gain the russet summit as the light fades from a summer sky. It is not so long ago that the road winding up from Bala to Ffestiniog – the B4391 – was narrow and rough-edged. Much of it has now been widened and straightened, and re-routed to go around Tryweryn Reservoir. The western part of it now goes down Cwm Prysor to Trawsfynydd; it is re-designated the A4212.

There was much opposition to the building of the reservoir here by Liverpool Corporation. Many old farms, cottages and a church have disappeared beneath the rising water, but today the artificial lake is filled, used to maintain the level of water in the River Dee on its way from Bala to the sea. The reservoir adds interest hereabouts, now that most of the spoil is over-grown and the works taken away. The view over Tryweryn towards Arenig Fach from the side of the impounding wall is pretty indeed, a single rowan by the road adding verticality to much horizontality.

Moel Llyfnant (2,461 ft) from the south

The single track railway which serpentined from the lower Conwy Valley, up the Lledr Valley to Blaenau-Ffestiniog and Ffestiniog crossed this wild area by way of Cwm Prysor and reached 1,300 feet at lonely Cwm Prysor station, then down the Tryweryn Valley to Bala. Today the line is closed but the old track which winds up Cwm Prysor from Trawsfynydd to Uwchmynydd (map reference: 816395) has been widened and re-surfaced in connection with the construction of the new reservoir.

In former days Cwm Prysor was a lonely off-shoot of a valley of scattered upland farms, and here was born and brought up the shepherd-poet Ellis Evans. He it was who wrote the long poem which won the premier award in the National Eisteddfod of 1917 under the pseudonym of Hedd Wyn. Only after he had been fatally injured in the Great War in the same year was the true identity of Hedd Wyn discovered. A statue to his memory stands overlooking the narrow main street in Trawsfynydd.

Ddualt (2,155 ft) from below Moel Llyfnant, looking south

THE ROUTE

1. A good starting point for the ascent of Arenig Fawr is the place called Pont-Rhyd-y-fen (map reference: 820394) where the river is crossed. Making up the steep and shadowed northern flanks of the mountain it is best to keep to the broken ground called Craig yr Hyrddod on the right and so gain the narrowing summit cone at about 2,500 feet. Continuing southwards the triangulation station upon the top is reached, about 1,700 feet higher than the starting point and a mile and three-quarters away, as measured on the map.

2. From the summit we now make northwards the way we have come, soon descending towards the north-east and so to the gap in the steep and broken ground which overlooks Llyn Arenig Fawr. The easiest way down to this almost circular lake is to follow the stream which runs down off the hill to join the lake near its south-western point. In misty weather some difficulty may be had in locating this stream, care being taken to avoid the broken ground right along this flank.

3. At the lake-side, often a dark place on account of its position in relation to the mountain, follow the western shore northwards and over the rocky shoulder called Gelli-deg and so down to the valley again and over Pont Rhyd-y-fen to the main road. Turn now for about three-quarters of a mile along the road towards Bala.

At a corner where there is a barn on the northern side of the road cross the boundary wall and ascend the even slopes to the shoulder called Y Foel and so easily upwards over heather, sedge and broken rocks to the open top of Arenig Fach (the Little Arenig). The ascent of 1,100 feet from the road takes me about three-quarters of an hour, and from the top in clear weather there are wide and surprising views of Snowdonia.

The northern prospect is away over the wide moorland dotted with standing water and streams to Yspytty-Ifan and the infant Conwy River. This rarely-trodden bog and heather land of Migneint is very reminiscent of Pennine moorland, acid wet-lands and scurrying cloud-shadows.

4. There are surprisingly near views of the Snowdon group from this hill-top, and of Tryweryn Reservoir. Let us return another way – down

to the north-east, avoiding the great and broken cliffs overlooking Llyn Arenig Fach. A descent of 750 feet brings one to the northern tip of this lake, a lake smaller (as it should be) than the lake beneath the bigger Arenig's eastern flank. By skirting the western shore, close beneath that cliff slope, we can contour southwards under Y Foel and so reach the road by the barn in a little more than an hour.

Try and arrange this ramble on a fine and sunny day as these are hills the views from which make them all the more fascinating, and, as the artist James Dickson Innes well knew, memorable and alluring, maybe disturbing. They are so to me.

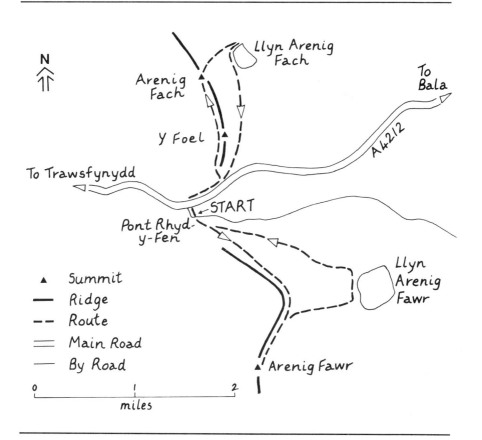

Summit View

Here upon the summit is an interesting memorial to those killed when an aircraft crashed on this mountain; quartz is embedded in concrete. This summit has other interesting connections too. In 1910 Augustus John invited his fellow-painter James Dickson Innes to join him on a painting expedition. They journeyed and painted in this area north-west of Bala, the region exercising a strange fascination upon Innes. His peculiar paintings of these uplands have been called "quietly dramatic" and completely in character with their "brooding solitudes".

It is recorded that, under Arenig Fawr's summit cairn, Innes buried certain letters in a silver casket. This mountain exercised such a strong influence upon him and his work that he wished to die upon its summit. Yes! Arenig Fawr is a mountain just like that – a "brooding solitude" of a place with views of far hills and far skies and other-worlds just out of sight.

James Dickson Innes (born incidentally, at Llanelly in 1887) died at the outbreak of the Great War only fours years or so after finding this wonderful and influential world which influenced so much of his later work.

From the summit cairn, one looks westwards to the far, eastern faces of the Harlech Dome and, to the north of west, towards the hidden wooded Vale of Ffestiniog. Between us and that valley-trough lies Tomen-y-Mur, the site of an important Roman fort overlooking Trawsfynydd Lake. There are fragments of walls and traces of a road. Nearby are the remains of a Roman Amphitheatre (map reference: 708389). Within the area of the fort is a mound, presumably the mound upon which a Norman castle of wood was erected. The Norman overlords would need any defence they could find in this wild land of jealous, resolute Celtic post-Roman earthworks to construct their buildings.

Sarn Helen ran past Tomen-y-Mur, the great Roman route from Caerhun (Conovium) in the lower Conwy Valley to Pennal in south Merionethshire. Much of this route can be followed still, notably in the wide valley of the Afon Eden.

Chapter 10

THE ROUND OF CNICHT AND THE MOELWYNS

Route: Croesor – Cnicht – Llyn Croesor – Moelwyn Mawr -Moelwyn Bach – Croesor

Distance: 7.5 miles

Grade: Moderately strenuous

Starting point: Croesor (map reference: 630447)

Maps: Ordnance Survey "Landranger" (1:50,000) Sheet 115 (Snowdon and Surrounding Area); Ordnance Survey "Outdoor Leisure" (1:25,000) Sheets 17 (Snowdonia – Snowdon and Conwy Valley Areas) and 18 (Snowdonia – Harlech and Bala Areas).

My first conscious contact with this massif goes back many years to a warm and hazy summer's day, actually it was late afternoon, when we drove along the hill road from Bala to Ffestiniog. As my father drove us down the steep road which descends into Ffestiniog and the Vale beneath (after contouring above the impressive gorge of the Afon Cynfa below Pont yr Afon Gam) the grey-blue silhouette of a mountain mass filled our view in front. No details of the mountain slopes upon which we looked were visible, only the great, blue bulk and the undulating ridge between three summits. Was it the Snowdon Horseshoe, the great cirque of Crib Goch, Y Wyddfa and Lliwedd? I wondered, and still was not sure, for where was the fourth summit of Crib y Ddisgl? It looked for all the world like the Snowdon massif seen from an unusual angle.

Of course, as we drove down the Vale of Ffestiniog towards the sea and the sunlight illuminated the slopes now coming into view, it became obvious that this was, in fact, a mountain group little known to me in those youthful days of exploding enthusiasm for all wild places – the Moelwyns. Three summits seen from the hill road above Ffestiniog are Moelwyn Bach (the little white hill), Moelwyn Mawr (the big white hill), and, to the north-east, Moel-yr-hydd (the stag's hill). Behind them when viewed from this point stands Cnicht, a long ridge running south-

westwards off the lake-dotted, swampy upland which culminates in
Moel Siabod in the north. This ridge drops, sharp and steep, from the
2,265 feet high summit and when viewed from the low land to the
south-west the steep ridge gives the false impression of a beautiful
conical mountain. Viewed from this angle Cnicht does indeed look like
the "Matterhorn of Wales", a title it has long enjoyed; but it is a fake, a
mountain to disappoint the moment one reaches its summit from the
south-west ridge and looks along the broad and level shoulder to little
lakes and broken ground beyond the cairn. Cnicht means, by the way,
"the knight" and I can't help feeling that the name is perfect for the
mountain looks every bit a knight in the true Arthurian sense.
Sometimes place-names fit without an easy explanation as to the reason
why, and here is a good example.

Nevertheless, the ascent of Cnicht and the continuation on to the
neighbouring Moelwyns makes an interesting and varied day, with
wonderful views of sea, estuary, lakes and other mountains.

The best way is up the long lane to the isolated village of Croesor, a lane

Cnicht (2,265 ft) from the ridge above Croesor

which leaves the road between Penrhyndeudraeth and Beddgelert and passes beneath a well proportioned gate-house complete with arch (map reference: 614421). The lane soon approaches the fine mansion of Plasbrondanw, former home of the late Sir Clough Williams-Ellis, architect, artist and patron of everything beautiful in his native Wales. This wonderful old house was badly damaged by fire some years ago, and a memory of that fire is preserved in the "Hanging Gardens" to the right of the house and high above the lane, a pedestal-supported urn contains ashes from the burnt habitation and a stone tablet recalls the skill of local craftsmen in rebuilding Plasbrondanw from those ashes.

Higher up still, above the trees and water-spouts of the "Hanging Gardens" stands a sham ruin, a folly in the traditional romantic style, which overlooks the level lands of the now-dry Traeth Mawr to the south-west. Across those reclaimed flat-lands rises the dry and rocky peninsula on which stands Castelldeudraeth, the noble-fronted former home of the Earl (Bertrand) Russell. Just beyond, at the edge of the peninsula, stands Port Meirion which is a reconstructed village in the Italian style, a folly of blue and white and turquoise created by Clough Williams-Ellis. All his works hereabouts bear a special quality of other-worldliness, of being part of a fairy tale which has partly come true.

The Route

Two miles up the lane beyond Plasbrondanw we come to Croesor, an unusual village where the lane ends beneath the great cone of Cnicht. Here lives the mountain writer Showell Styles; and here, too, lived the great Welsh historian Bob Owen. His small house was filled with books, his memory perpetuated in a village seat made from local slate and designed by Sir Clough Williams-Ellis. Pilgrims come to Croesor to see the home and memorial to Bob Owen.

1. The best way to ascend Cnicht is to continue along the lane to Croesor-fawr (map reference: 639452) then cross the old mineral trackway and cross the river, the Afon Croesor, by a slab bridge of slates.

2. The way winds up the steepening flanks and onto the obvious ridge and so in $1^1/_2$ hours from the bottom the summit is gained. Near the top, a steep section of exposed rock is turned on the right by a relatively easy scramble over natural rock steps.

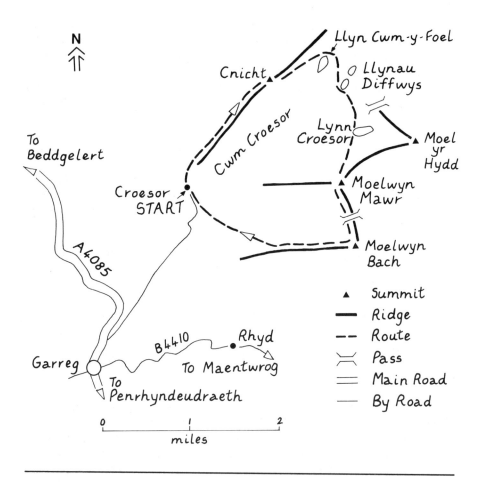

On the 2,265 feet summit, Moel Hebog appears quite close to the west over the void of the Glaslyn. Beyond lie the other hills of this lovely but neglected range. To the north the Snowdon group is also surprisingly near and below the waters of Llyn Dinas are visible in lower Nant Gwynant, three miles away.

3. Continuing along the main axis of our mountain we go down the north-east ridge a short distance and then steeply down to the little elongated lake unnamed on the Ordnance Survey map through which flows the Afon Cwm-y-foel – and which I like to call Llyn Cwm-y-foel. The descent is over steep grass and broken rocks and the inexperienced rambler must take great care here. In poor visibility this descent can be dangerous and one may prefer to continue along the ridge northwards until an easier and smoother way down presents itself. In any event it is best to decide one's route ahead from the top of Cnicht, over the broken and misleading ground between here and Moelwyn Mawr. It is a strange, forsaken land.

4. After skirting my little Llyn Cwm-y-foel we reach the twin lakes called Llynnau Diffwys. Beyond them we reach an old quarry track which winds round above the head of Cwm Croesor and seems to end mysteriously well beneath the summit of Cnicht. Following it we reach a world of true desolation, a "ghost town" of derelict quarry buildings and piled slates.

It is easy to imagine great activity here in the days when slate was extracted from these hill-tops at great cost and inconvenience. Slate became the premier roofing material during the spread of railways in the second half of the last century, and much of the great quantity of slates quarried in this elevated and difficult country around Blaenau Ffestiniog was sent down to Portmadog by railway to be shipped all over Britain and the world. With the decline in the domestic consumption of roofing slate during this century these remoter quarries fell into decay and were finally closed. Here is a typical example.

5. And so, on up the even slopes to the south-west, passing little Llyn Croesor, and eventually to the 2,527 feet high top of Moelwyn Mawr. The slopes are grassy with steep scree falling away to the right, down towards Cwm Croesor. Here on the breezy top of the higher Moelwyn there are fine views in every direction in clear weather. Particularly interesting is the one to the south-west, to the wide flats of Traeth Mawr and the mouth of the Afon Glaslyn.

6. Our route now lies down the south ridge towards Moelwyn Bach – alternatively one can shorten the walk by descending the south-west ridge for over two miles to Croesor.

7. On our way to Moelwyn Bach we go over an intermediate summit which looks like a separate hill from the highest Moelwyn. Down now beyond this intermediate peak to the pass where a winding quarry road goes – seen earlier from the top of Moelwyn Mawr. Steeply down on our left the grey waters of Llyn Stwlan can be seen, its level raised by a large dam wall which took great skill to erect at this altitude and in such an inaccessible position. The impounding wall can be seen to advantage from many places upon the eastern sides of the Vale of Ffestiniog.

8. From the pass it is best to go up the grass slope which lies immediately to the left of an extensive scree slope which drops from high up on Moelwyn Bach when seen from Moelwyn Mawr. High up on this scree a large slab of rock forms a remarkably regular square when seen from the higher hill.

9. So to the 2,334 feet summit of the lesser Moelwyn, reached in approximately one hour from the greater Moelwyn. Looking down to the north-east is the cwm containing Llyn Stwlan and, behind, the sixth highest summit of this group called Moel-yr-hydd (2,124 feet) hiding the third highest, Allt fawr (2,287 feet) – the great slope – from our view. Steeply down to the east lies the complicated grey – the only word for it – which is Ffestiniog slate workings extending from Tan-y-grisiau and Bethania, up onto the elephantine form of Manod Mawr and northwards through Rhiwbryfdir and almost to the top of the Crimea Pass at 1,263 feet above sea level where the road goes over to the Conwy Valley.

10. Descending, now we go down the long westward-pointing ridge and at about 1,500 feet (about three-quarters of a mile below the top) it is best to turn down towards the north-west, into the hollow drained by the Afon Maesgwm and so round and down to Croesor. This hollow is ill-drained and at or after dusk, care must be exercised to avoid the wettest areas.

Choose, when possible, a bright day of open skies and sunshine, and this circuit will remain in the memory forever.

The Estuary

Two centuries ago, a great estuary came to the sea here at the "corner" where the coastline turns westwards to form the Lleyn peninsula's southern shore. The Afon Glaslyn draining its mountain valley from the north and the Afon Dwyryd draining the lovely Vale of Ffestiniog join here and had a tremendous joint mouth which extended about five miles across its mouth from Harlech to the present position of Portmadog. Running down the middle of this comparatively mighty estuary a narrow and rocky peninsula separates the two rivers, terminating in the little headland of Trwynypenrhyn (map reference: 580370).

Longshore drift up Cardigan Bay caused the formation of Morfa Harlech, that great triangle of sand-dunes and naturally reclaimed land behind them. Harlech Point at the extreme northern end of Morfa Harlech now reaches to within less than three-quarters of a mile of the rocky northern shore of the estuary's present mouth. Man has also played a big part in the reduction of the waters of the estuary, principally one inventive man – W. A. Madocks.

Sir John E. Lloyd has described how before the nineteenth century travellers had to cover a considerable mileage to avoid the waters and extensive tidal sands of the twin estuaries. From Harlech one crossed the Afon Dwyryd by the graceful and ancient bridge at Maentwrog, then took the sinuous road that clings to the eastern edge of the Traeth Mawr, crossing the Afon Glaslyn by the famous bridge at Pont Aber Glaslyn with its well-known northward view of a conifer-clung canyon. Finally, the road southwards down the other shore of the estuary led round to Criccieth. Indeed, "the fertile lands of Lleyn and Eifionydd were cut off from Merionethshire and Llanrwst by impassable roads and the perils of the Traeth."

As early as 1625 Sir John Wynn of Gwydir, near Llanrwst, had the idea that this great waste of tidal water might be drained and the marshland reclaimed. W. A. Madocks bought the Tanrallt estate in 1798 and, by way of an experiment, drained an area at the eastern side of the estuary which became known as the Penmorfa Flats – enclosed originally by an embankment which ran northwards from the present site of Portmadog to the village of Prenteg. On the edge of some of this reclaimed land, in the shelter and shadow of the long escarpment known as Alltwen (the Tremadoc Bluffs or Rocks where rock climbers have in recent years made many routes), a site was chosen for a completely new market town called Tremadoc. This settlement has never become more than a pretentious village, famed for its wide and well-planned main street and as being the birthplace of Lawrence of Arabia.

By an Act of Parliament passed in 1808 a long embankment was planned and erected right across the mouth of the Traeth Mawr, so enclosing an area of about 3,000 acres which was drained, save for a small lake where wild fowl come in winter, sheltered from the sea winds by the embankment itself.

Portmadog, upon the northern bank of the Traeth Mawr, owes its development and subsequent growth to the opening of the railway from Ffestiniog's slate quarries in 1836. The port grew to become the main town in this district, named (like Tremadoc) after the industrious and far-sighted W. A. Madocks, though recent research suggests that he really named these places after the legendary twelfth-century Madoc who is said to have found America after sailing from a rock in the Traeth Mawr. Today one can travel a comparatively short distance between Harlech and Portmadog by using the toll bridge over the Afon Dwyryd and the Traeth Mawr.

And so from our extensive viewpoint upon the higher Moelwyn we see a converted landscape, or rather a landscape with a detail converted; dry land where there was tidal estuary of wet sand or, at full tide, shining sea between rugged slopes and short-stemmed woods of native oak.

Chapter 11

THE LOVELY LAND OF LLEYN

Criccieth and David Lloyd George – Conical hills and antiquities -The Rivals – Morfa Nefyn and Port Dinllaen – Around Aberdaron – Mynydd Mawr and Bardsey.

Route: Llanaelhaearn – Tre'r Ceiri – Highest Summit – Bwlch yr Eifl – Llanaelhaearn

Distance: 4.5 miles

Grade: Moderate

Starting Point: Llanaelhaearn (map reference: 388448)

Map: Ordnance Survey "Landranger" (1:50,000) Sheet 123 (Lleyn).

Surely, one could spend a century in the wonderful green cove and hill land which is Lleyn and still wish that one knew more of its many charms. The Lleyn peninsula is the term normally used but really "lleyn" is enough for that means, in fact "peninsula".

Seen from the south, from the shores of Cardigan Bay at Barmouth or Llanbedr on a clear day or when the summer sun sinks fiercely beyond those northern peninsular hills of great grace, one sees a promised land pointing out far to the west, only to slide eventually into the western sea; to reappear again in one last effort as the little island of Bardsey with its romantic history and cold, interrupted warning light.

The colour of Lleyn is blue, deep mauve-blue when clouds ride upon or over the conical hills, light and freshly blue when the sun shines from an open sky. In certain conditions of lighting the hills appear to ride above the intervening water of Cardigan Bay and Bardsey seems to hover clear of the restless water at the end of the peninsula; a fascinating phenomenon due to the refraction of light.

For me, Criccieth is the southern portal to Lleyn, a quiet and romantic place by the sea with innumerable associations. There is a ruined castle upon its seaside rock, a castle referred to as being the prison of

Gruffydd, the son of Llywelyn ap Iorwerth, in 1239. It was one of the old pre-Edwardian castles of North Wales, but after 1282 Edward I held the land and built new castles like Beaumaris and modified old castles like Criccieth. In 1283 and 1284 the King stayed here on a number of occasions but it remained a secondary fortress, it being recorded that £306 were spent upon the castle in 1292 compared with £8,177 upon Harlech Castle. The Engine Tower at the north-eastern corner of the castle overlooks the town and is believed to have housed a machine for hurling stones upon invaders by means of a catapult. The castle was more advanced than certain other pre-Edwardian castles, like Dolbadarn, and had at least one fine room with carvings.

The Black Prince became the owner in 1343, to be taken over by the great Welsh hero Owain Glyndwr in 1404. In less than half a century the castle lay in ruins and has remained so ever since, slowly crumbling at the onslaught of sea spray, wind and rain.

Criccieth is linked forever with David Lloyd George, Earl Lloyd George of Dwyfor as he later became. Though born in Manchester (in January 1863) he came at an early age to live with his uncle Richard Lloyd in the lovely village of Llanystumdwy on the banks of the Afon Dwyfor, two miles to the west of Criccieth.

The cottage where he spent his youth is still inhabited, standing close by the main road where now holiday traffic thunders by, towards the holiday camps and massed ranks of caravans beyond. Lloyd George died at his lovely old Llanystumdwy home called Ty Newydd, only a short distance from his uncle's cottage, in March 1945. He lies buried in a beautiful site above the wooded glade of the Dwyfor, where he used to sit and contemplate the peace and unity of nature, qualities he would dearly have liked to bestow on the world of politics and government which he knew so well in later life.

His daughter, Lady Megan Lloyd George, lived in a fine, white house on the upper lane between Criccieth and Llanystumdwy and David Lloyd George's brother, William George – the oldest practising solicitor in Britain – died in February, 1967 at his Criccieth home aged over one hundred and one years.

Lleyn has a quantity of hills along its length fascinatingly conical in form. Most are separated one from another by undulating, sometimes wooded and recessed, pastoral country. There are many foxes in this most suitable region and the Lleyn and Eifionydd Fox Destruction Society was formed in 1964 to control their numbers. One pound was offered for each adult fox brush and ten shillings for each cub tail. Upon many of these conical heights men of former times lived or worked or retreated in dangerous times. There are many remains of these Lleyn inhabitants still to be seen; hill forts, burial cairns and standing stones.

Close to the main road from Caernarfon to Pwllheli, to the east of it near to the cross-roads called Four Crosses, is an ancient standing stone and burial chamber. Whether these two relics have any original connection cannot be proven, but it would seem that they are the remains of a belief of the living and a memorial to the dead respectively, looking out upon the shallow and well-watered valley of the southward-flowing Afon Erch.

To the north-east, by about two and a half miles, Carn Pentyrch stands as a mound on top of a smooth-sided mound almost 750 feet above sea level -burial mound or defensive site for a forgotten family who grazed their cattle upon the rolling hills of eastern Lleyn before the Romans came.

Then there are the standing stones in the marshlands below Moelypenmaen three miles north-west of Pwllheli, and the secret ruins of Garn Bodvan upon the 918 feet high wood-encircled top of the conical hill overlooking Tan-y-graig (map reference: 312393). Upon the next conical hill to the south-west are the remains of Carn Fadrun at 1,217 feet and occupying a bare and craggy viewpoint, wilder and more severe than the neighbour.

Over the next conical hill, Garn Bach – the little rock or hill or hill-top mound – and onto the next stands another antiquity called Garn Saethon.

Six miles to the south we reach the southern-most finger of Lleyn – the Lizard of this peninsula – where high grasslands swell up in Mynydd Cilan to give sea cliffs reaching to 385 feet in height. Near the southern tip is a burial chamber close to Cilan Uchaf Farm. On a sunny day of wind and broken cumulus and dappled seas we walked from the road-head and by the burial chamber's remains to look out over the rock-and-sand girt bay called Porth Ceiriad to the neighbouring headland of Trwyn yr Wylfa. The words uttered by King Beowulf as he lay dying by the sea seemed appropriate:

> *Tell the famed fighters*
> *To raise on the headland*
> *A bright barrow over me*
> *After my burning.*

Out on our summer headland, we could just see the little island of St. Tudwal's West. Upon the larger St. Tudwal's East are the remains of St. Tudwal's Chapel, on the smaller isle is a lighthouse, marking the dangers of these rocks and isles and headlands to vessels, especially sailing vessels, plying in St. Tudwal's Road off-shore from Abersoch.

As we walked on westwards round the southernmost tip of this southernmost point of Lleyn red valerian waved in the wind off the sea and a pair of herring gulls called on the wing out over space. The place was full of peace, a noisesome peace of watery sounds, the sea wind and sea birds and red valerian crossing stems with flowering grass stalks. I set to wondering who had walked our way when the hills to the north were inhabited by the builders of Carn Fadrun and the scores of other ancient sites, known and unknown.

Peace-loving herdsmen and cultivators of sparse places they definitely were, only driven to defending their possessions and themselves when hard times or greed caused strangers to move in their direction. Then circumstances forced them to the hilltops, which they fortified.

On the western side of this southernmost tip, grass, short-clipped by sheep, falls steeply to hidden cliffs – 250 feet cliffs completely out of sight below the lowest flange of the grass slope. Soon we rise to the 385 feet triangulation station and can look westwards over the three-mile length of Porth Neigwl. This wide bay with its fine, unspoilt beach is normally referred to as Hell's Mouth, a dangerous place for vessels, and where the south-west wind can rage in, bringing much wreckage to litter the long beach.

Overlooking Porth Neigwl on the western side rises Mynydd Rhiw, only one foot short of 1,000 feet. At the northern end of this hill are the fascinating remains of a Stone Axe Factory, a place where the ancient inhabitants of Lleyn used the hard stone to fashion axe-heads. On the slopes dropping to Porth Neigwl are the remains of a Long Cairn – where communal burials once took place. To the south, near Rhiw, is another burial chamber.

In north-eastern Lleyn, where the peninsula widens to become part of the body of North Wales, is the upland rectangle with five summits at its perimeter. In the col between the western summits of Gurn Goch and Gurn Ddu are ruined burial cairns and on the 1,270 feet top of Pen-y-gaer is an earthwork suggesting a defensive site similar to that more important remain upon the Rivals.

The loveliest of all Lleyn's hills are indeed the group known as Yr Eifl -the Rivals. They rise sharply from the sea, from Caernarfon Bay, and are best seen from south-western Anglesey or the mainland coast towards Caernarfon, or away to the south-west at Morfa Nefyn. I know of no more beautiful British mountain form than that of Yr Eifl from these viewpoints in certain lighting conditions.

Three domes upon the sky,
Blue and darker blue they go,
Between sunset and I.

The highest top lies properly between the two lesser summits and at 1,849 feet is the highest point of Lleyn (see route description at end of chapter).

The summits of Yr Eifl are seen to tremendous advantage from the resort of Morfa Nefyn – a quiet, pre-war place with a lovely bay and the glint of small sails out to sea. Porth Dinllaen is the name of this wide bay and enclosing it on the west is the narrow peninsula of Trwyn Porth Dinllaen. I can think of few more interesting seaside spots, with rocks and a pre-historic promontory fort, a blow-hole where the tide rushes in under the golf links and a lifeboat station. I remember an early June day when we first discovered that headland, a promontory of warm, sheep-cropped grass and thrift in full bloom, dotting the rocks with pink. Overhead the herring gulls were wheeling and a lone oyster catcher "bleeped" as it winged westwards towards a few white castles of cloud, then I dozed in the utter peace of that long-ago headland. Is it still quite the same place?

From the white-and-blue hotel above the road to the beach and Porth Dinllaen one can look across to the old inn and cottages of Porth Dinllaen, a smugglers retreat if ever I saw one, but now the cottages are bright holiday retreats.

Aberdaron Bay is the westernmost bay of any size on the south coast of Lleyn and the ancient village of Aberdaron overlooks its bay, the "Penzance of Lleyn". This village is liberally washed with white, a clean and quite unspoilt place close to western seas. There is a fine walk round the bay to the steep inlet of Porth Meudwy, keeping above the rocks. Here in late summer the Everlasting Pea covers the slopes with pink blooms. Down at the edge of Porth Meudwy the boats lie about and a Standard Fordson tractor used to stand by to haul up the lobster boats when required.

It is from here that one can get a vessel to carry one to Bardsey. The best viewpoint from which to see this outpost island of Lleyn is the extreme western headland of the peninsula, called Mynydd Mawr – literally, the Big Mountain. The lane winds on westwards passing white-washed cottages and farms crouching low against the sea wind. On either side of the serpentine route are bocage walls, stones and turf piled as a solid rampart in which grows a wide variety of wild flora, predominant in early summer being the foxglove. Bocage boundaries are typical of far western Europe, including Brittany, Cornwall, Pembrokeshire, western North Wales, western Eire and the Hebrides – all Celtic lands facing the sea.

The little lane ends beneath the 524 feet summit of Mynydd Mawr. The slaty rock forms sloping slabs of pink and all about is Western Gorse, a lower and compacter form of the Common Gorse. The yellow blooms contrast well with the bright mauve of ling and heather in late summer, a truly wild rock garden area.

On top of the headland is a Coast Guard look-out, from where a wide ocean view can be had and Bardsey appears across the ruffled Bardsey Sound just over two miles to the south-west. On the stony grassland below the Coast Guard look-out the small forms of Carline Thistle dot the ground, seemingly everlasting in type and reminiscent of the Alpine Silverthistle of high, scree slopes and dry Alps. On the slope towards Bardsey is Saint Mary's Well, a Holy well associated with the Holy island across the Sound.

Fortunately, much of Mynydd Mawr is National Trust property so that this particular height is safe from the ingress of caravans and holiday chalets and sporadic development.

Bardsey or Yyns Enlii – "the island in the current" of the ancient Welsh – is a holy island, sacred ever since Einion Frenin founded a religious centre there in A.D. 420. For six hundred years thereafter it became a place of pilgrimage, three visits equalling one visit to Rome.

Bardsey Island from the end of Lleyn

Beneath the western slopes of Bardsey's highest hill, called Mynydd Enlii – "the Mountain of the Current" – are the ruins of Saint Mary's Abbey, marked by the remains of a thirteenth-century tower and a cross shaft which was carved during the sixth century.

There are 20,000 saints buried here at the northern end of the island, according to tradition; this may well be a fact as it is known that over one thousand monks from Bangor Iscoed came here for refuge after the Battle of Chester.

Why are the remains of such an important abbey so few? Much of the stone was used to build the modern buildings erected by the island's owner, Sir Spencer Bulkley Wynn, after 1870.

Cristin Farm also shelters beneath the western slope of Mynydd Enlii, a model farm when built and now the Bird and Field Observatory, which is open annually from March to October for the study of natural history. The Irish Sea is a regular route for migrating birds *en route* for, or leaving, their breeding grounds. Four thousand pairs of shearwaters breed here upon Bardsey, together with colonies of guillemots, kittiwakes and razorbills upon the limited area of sea cliffs.

The island consists of two parts, the northernmost being larger and higher, the southernmost being small and rising to only 66 feet above sea level. The largest bay is that which almost divides the island into two and is called Porth Henllwyn, where is situated the small anchorage sheltered from the western seas by the isthmus 15 feet above the sea joining north to south. Here one disembarks from the motor boat which plies weekly from Aberdaron when wind and sea permit.

Near the centre of the low-lying southern part of Bardsey stands the famous lighthouse, exhibiting an important light over the Irish Sea. Protection for passing sea birds has been placed on the lighthouse, to prevent the successively attracted-then-blinded birds from flying into the lantern. Before such protection many migratory birds were lost each year from this cause.

Lord Newborough was buried on Bardsey in 1888 and a Celtic cross marks his grave. It is appropriate to end a visit to Lleyn's lovely land with this last far and isolated island where, upon Lord Newborough's grave, are carved the words:

Safe in this island
Where each saint would be,
How wilt thou smile
On life's stormy sea.

The Route

1. Llanaelhaearn is the proper starting place for exploring the Rivals, sheltering in their evening shadow to the east of the trinity of cones. A lane leads up over the grassy eastern shoulder of the 1,591 feet eastern height. At the highest point of this lane, at about six hundred feet above sea level, turn up the steep, grassy ridge. In less than a thousand feet of ascent is the sudden summit, reached in about fifty minutes.

We are on the slate-surrounded cairn and in clear conditions we realise that we are surrounded by a "something", a rampart over which we have scrambled without really noticing it. We are in Tre'r Ceiri – the Town of Giants – a fortification erected by the hardy Ordovices and occupied during the centuries of Roman occupation. The wild situation was chosen, as on other Lleyn hill-tops, as it offered a good look-out over a wide area.

The cattle, goats and sheep could graze the lower slopes and be watched from the rampart above. Small hut circles are scattered around the hill's flat top in a haphazard fashion, typical of constructions of that period, a dwelling being erected where building materials were most conveniently to hand. Around Tre'r Ceiri's dwellings the rampart was erected, a well-built wall with a step on the inside, presumably for sentries to parade in times of danger from attack.

On the way up we were able to look over to the north-west, to the 1,458 feet high north-western summit – where there are the remains of a burial mound. This hill has been almost quarried away, only a conical summit is left and sharp steps scar the northern face.

2. From this first summit we drop to the heathery col leading to the highest central summit. On the sides of the col I am reminded of the place called the Gap on St. Kilda, between Oiseval and Conachair. In half an hour the 1,849 feet summit is gained with wide views on every side.

On sunny days the pink rock in the old quarries makes a pleasing contrast with the blue-green waters far below and beyond. I could spend a long, long time on this lofty viewpoint, picking out all the well-loved hills and bays and valleys from such an unusual angle. Lleyn is a summer land and no less this, its highest point. Choose a still summer day and this experience will never be forgotten.

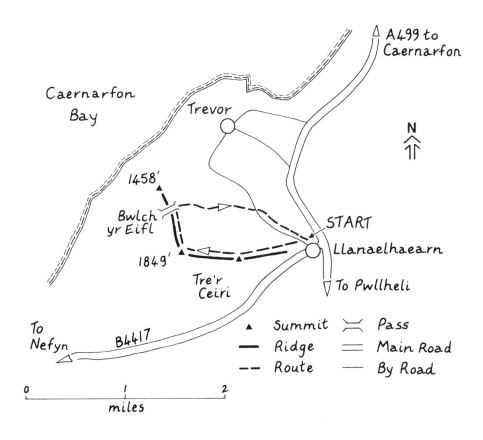

3. The 1,458 feet north-western summit hangs directly above Caernarfon Bay and the scramble to its top is well worth the effort but the right-of-way up to it is disputed. If you venture to the little summit there's a fine view down to the south-west, directly into the deep valley of Nant Gwrtheyrn. Down there is the former quarry village called Porth-y-nant -remains of old piers jutting seawards remind us that most of the rock was exported by sea.

The quarries became uneconomic and the terraced houses forming a sort of square shaded by tall trees, the manager's house and Capel Seilo (built 1878) were left to decay. As recently as 1964 one house along the terrace was inhabited by a coastguard and his sister. Porth-y-nant has now ben rebuilt as a Welsh language centre.

On a summer's evening long ago we walked down through the bracken of this secret valley as the sun set in a pale orange glow over the sea. Bats flew between the terraced houses, one had the feeling of walking in a dead spa, a lifeless Bath or Buxton. The light faded suddenly and in the warm darkness we went up out of the valley by the hairpin track as the stars began to shine over the Rivals.

4. Back on Bwlch yr Eifl, north of the highest summit, a path goes down to the north and joins the narrow lane which leads back to Llanael-haearn. From Bwlch Eifl one can be on the lane where we started out in about forty minutes.

Unrivalled belvedere – Caernarfon Bay from The Rivals

Chapter 12

UPON THE MOEL HEBOG MASSIF

Route: Pennant – Moel Hebog – Moel Ogof – Moel Lefn -Trum-y-Ddysgl – Mynydd Drws-y-coed – Trum-y-Ddysgl – Mynydd Tal-y-Mignedd -Garnedd-goch – Mynydd Craig-goch – Cwm Ciprwth – Pennant

Distance: 16.5 miles.

Grade: Strenuous

Starting Point: Pennant (map reference: 531469)

Maps: Ordnance Survey "Landranger" (1:50,000) Sheet 115 (Snowdon and Surrounding Area); Ordnance Survey "Outdoor Leisure" (1:25,000) Sheet 17 (Snowdonia – Snowdon and Conwy Valley Areas).

Moel Hebog is the mountain which dominates the lovely Vale of Gwynant, a mountain best seen from the Vale's floor, by the waters of Llyn Gwynant or Llyn Dinas – admittedly a distant view but a balanced one; a mountain often looks at its finest from some distance and Moel Hebog is no exception. It dominates the lower (the western) end of the Vale of Gwynant, at its joining with the less lovely Vale of Colwyn. The Afon Glaslyn drains Gwynant and turns southwards at the place where it collects the waters of the Afon Colwyn, to flow through that well-known National Trust gorge called the Pass of Aberglaslyn shown on a thousand post card views, and finally out over the reclaimed lands of Traeth Mawr and so to Cardigan Bay's north-eastern corner.

At the confluence of the Afon Colwyn with the dominant Afon Glaslyn – where the latter changes its general direction – stands the ancient village of Beddgelert.

In the churchyard of Beddgelert is the grave of Owen Glendower's friend, Rhys Goch, buried here five and a half centuries ago, but a more

Mynydd Drws-y-Coed (centre) from the Beddgelert path to Snowdon

famous grave, by tradition, stands in the flat fields on the flood plain of the Afon Glaslyn a short distance south of the village. This is the grave of Gelert, hound of Llewelyn, "last" Prince of Wales. The legend is told at length on a tablet at the site of the grave; though Llewelyn himself died in 1282 and was buried at Cilmery, Builth Wells.

Wolves are said to have killed the Prince's infant son, reminding us of the fact that earlier, in Saxon times, King Edgar of England required the King of North Wales to pay tribute of three hundred wolf skins each year. It is recorded that this tribute was not paid for long as there were not sufficient wolves left in these mountains, and it is most unlikely that by the thirteenth century, by Prince Llewelyn's time, any wolves remained in what is now North Wales, so that the story of Gelert, the faithful hound, is only a legend.

About four miles downstream from Beddgelert, where the Afon Glaslyn now flows down the western side of the reclaimed flats of the Traeth Mawr is an old "island" reaching over 100 feet above sea level called Ynysfor – once a rocky isle in the great tidal estuary now virtually drained. Ynysfor means "the Big Island" and is the home of the famous Ynysfor Hunt, the only pack of foxhounds still in existence in the region and the oldest private pack in Wales, records of kills in the area dating from 1750. All other foxhound packs in the area have died out, including the Pwllheli, Tremadoc and Caernarfon packs. The Anglesey Hunt is now also defunct, due to the excessive expense of maintaining horses, but Anglesey still boasts its beagles.

The Ynysfor Hunt goes on foot, a necessity in the rough mountain region which is its country. Even in winter the hunt goes high and there are records of foxes having been killed on the high pass between Snowdon and Lliwedd, called Bwlch-y-Saethau. The former Master of the Hunt was Colonel John Jones, "John Peel of Merioneth", who was killed by a falling boulder by the falls of Pistyll Cain (where the Afon Gain joins the young Afon Mawddach) in 1948 while searching for a foxhound. Since then his nephew, Major Edmund Roche, has been Master of the Ynysfor.

The Route

1. Though Beddgelert is the traditional and proper place to start the ascent of Moel Hebog, a more satisfactory point is from somewhere in the large and relatively unknown valley drained by the Afon Dwyfor to the west of Moel Hebog, where the scattered settlements are known collectively as Pennant, and including the sparse village of Llanfihangel-y-pennant. Right round this basin, to east, north and west, rises high land forming a virtually continuous ridge and the route described here follows much of this watershed.

2. From the narrow lane winding up the Vale of Pennant there is an even slope of about 2,150 feet leading to the summit cairn of Moel Hebog ("the hill of the hawk"). In clear weather there is the sea to south and west, the woods and pastures of the Vales of Gwynant and Colwyn below us to the east, and, far to the north through the trench of the Afon Gwyrfai lies the Menai Straits and Anglesey beyond.

3. Down now to the north-west by an interesting scramble to the pass, or bwlch, of 1,750 feet separating Moel Hebog from the next summit on our

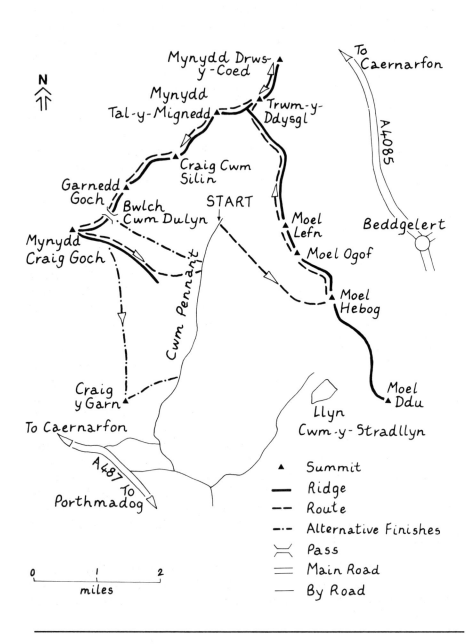

route, Moel Ogof. It is 2,020 feet high, but before making the short ascent to its round and broken top it is worth investigating the bold cliff quite high on the mountain's eastern face, overlooking the large forests in Cwm Meillionen (map reference: 560479). It is best to descend to the cliff from the pass and so reach it at a relatively high point at its southern side near the top of a steep gully. There a narrow gangway leads out onto the eastern face of the cliff – Craig Ogof, "the Cliff of the Cave" – and eventually to a dark recess.

Prince of Wales

Owen Glendower, leader of the last and most serious rebellion by the Welsh against the English, was proclaimed Prince of Wales and in 1404 captured Harlech Castle from Henry IV. As time went on, however, the English forces regained the whole of Wales and Glendower took to the mountains of north and central Wales, being cared for by his many staunch kinsmen who were to be found in every wild valley and on every mountainside where he roamed. It is very probable that for a considerable time he lived in this cave on Moel Ogof, eventually going into oblivion after 1412. Four years later Owen Glendower – to be accurate I should call him Owain Glyndwr – died in a remote corner of Herefordshire. It is a fine thing to scramble to this lonely cave and, looking out up the length of the Vale of Gwynant to graceful Moel Siabod ten miles to the north-east, imagine how that loyal Welshman lived here in solitude and poverty over five centuries ago; his cave is virtually unaltered, still the mosses and the ferns grow from cracks in the damp walls of his hiding-place.

This is Owen Glendower's Cave, the cave giving its name to both the cliff and hill itself. The cave is quite shallow, really an alcove well-draped with mosses and ferns.

4. Returning back along the gangway or terrace one passes the entrance to a smaller recess or cave. This is an asbestos "mine"! Asbestos, is by the way, a fibrous mineral and is normally found in veins associated with rocks rich in magnesia, notably serpentine. I believe it to be a fact that this is the only such "mine" in the British Isles. Many years ago asbestos was discovered oozing from the rock face here and attempts were made to extract it commercially. Such attempts proved abortive, and one can today crawl into the opening and pull out handfuls of the wet, raw asbestos from the "veins" sandwiched between the rock layers.

5. Return up the slope now direct to the summit of Moel Ogof and on towards the next hill of Moel Lefn (2,094 feet), a hill with three slight and adjacent tops which seem to contradict its meaning when translated – "the smooth hill".

6. Descending steeply now over much-broken terrain we gain the disused quarries at the head of Cwm Trwsgl. Down here is the 1,300 feet high pass where an ancient trackway goes over this watershed between the Vale of Pennant to the south-west and Rhyd-ddu to the north-west, at the western feet of the Snowdon massif.

This col is called Bwlch y Ddwyelor ("the pass of the clumsy hollows") and seems, to me, to have been most well named for if one looks about and down on either side, the hollow or cut or depression forming the pass gives a sense of being ragged or clumsy.

7. Proceeding to the north-west a little summit of 1,529 feet is passed, from which a good view is had of the ridge of fine hills which block the head of the Vale of Pennant from Mynydd Craig-goch (1,996 feet) at the far left (western end) of the ridge as we gaze to Trum-y-Ddysgl (2,329 feet) directly ahead up that mountain's south ridge, upon which we are now standing about 1.5 miles from the summit.

Westward prospect from Snowdon – the Nantlle valley and Mynydd Mawr

This fine rampart of hills looks down on the far side upon the valley of Nantlle and over towards the Irish Sea. They are lovely, little-trodden hills, full of special charm and unexpected thrills for the mountaineer. In height they do not compare with the high hills of central Snowdonia to the east but they are big for all that and must be treated with respect, even by the summer rambler.

8. Go up to the narrow ridge ahead and so northwards to the 2,329 feet top of Trum-y-Ddysgl – "the ridge of the dish" – which overlooks a steep-floored cwm on its northern flank, and which it almost surrounds with broken cliffs, hence the name given to the mountain. Far below the old road between Rhyd-ddu and Nantlle climbs over Bwlch Gylfin close to the small lakes at 770 feet above sea level called Llyn Bwlch-y-Moch and Llyn-y-Dywarchen wherein are good trout, though the fishing is private.

Across the valley, as we look northwards, rises the large bulk of Mynydd Mawr (2,290 feet) which has an almost frightening appearance in conditions of dull lighting and dark cloud. It seems elephantine or as a sleeping leviathan of the deep, notably from the eastern shore of Llyn Cwellyn on a miserable day. Its name ("the big mountain") suggests this, but its altitude is relatively modest. Facing us as we look are the broken cliffs dropping to steep screes, sparkling pink in bright sunshine. Actually the rocks forming this mountain are granitic, unusual in Snowdonia for there are few conspicuous granite features in the area. The rock is composed largely of dark-blue crystals formed from sodium-hornblende. These crystals have only been located in three or four locations in the British Isles.

These cliffs to which we look are Craig-y-Bere ("the kite's crag") and though they appear attractive to the climber they have never been popular on account of their rotten quality; much of the exposed granite comes away with a pull of the hand and so is dangerous.

9. Skirting above the north-facing cliffs there is some scrambling along the narrow ridge, then we reach the nearby summit of Mynydd Drws-y-coed (about seventy feet less than Trum-y-Ddysgl) and on, with more interesting progress on the narrow ridge, to the outlying summit of Y Garn (2,080 feet).

This spur presumably once possessed a burial mound or cairn (hence "the cairn") to some long-forgotten Welsh chieftain. The summit of Snowdon is less than four miles distant and exhibits its less well-known facade, curving up among wide cloud-shadows from Beddgelert and Rhyd-ddu as often as not.

10. Back now, over the top of Trum-y-Ddysgl and westwards on the grassy ridge separating Cwmyffynnon to the north and Cwmdwyfor to the south. Only 700 feet below our ridge-top, on the southern side, is the spring where the Afon Dwyfor is born before its descent of the Vale of Pennant to the sea west of Criccieth where Lloyd George lies at rest. It is only a mile to the top of neighbouring Mynydd Tal-y-mignedd, "the mount at the end of the bog". The highest point is crowned with a tall stone pillar built here by local quarrymen to mark the spot where the three castles at Caernarfon, Criccieth and Harlech can be seen.

The next summit lies to the south-west and exhibits a broken face to the rambler from where we stand. Its name is Craig Cwm Silin and it is 2,408 feet high. To gain it there is a steep drop to the intervening pass of Bwlch Dros-bern – literally, "the pass across the top" (of the Vale of Pennant) – which allows a medium-height route between Nantlle and the Vale of Pennant.

11. From the 1,640 feet pass there is another scramble to the top of Craig Cwm Silin. Proceeding slightly south of west a stony plateau is traversed, avoiding the steep cliffs towering above the Llynau Cwmsilin, cliffs which are now an important climbing ground of western Snowdonia.

12. Over a mile beyond the last summit we gain the 2,301 feet high top Carnedd-goch with its wall and triangulation station. This, "the red cairn", is a smooth-sided hill where the blasts of winter often roar in from the sea. Low cloud can make route-finding difficult beyond this top, but by aiming due south from the triangulation station one should reach the next pass (Bwlch Cwmdulyn) and so avoid the broken and rocky ground at the head of Cwm Dulyn to the west. Over this "pass of the hollow of the black lake" there is a good walking route between the Vale of Pennant and Llanllyfni to the west. From here the walk can be shortened by cutting straight down in Cwm Ciprwth and so to Pennant. If finished thus the route is 14.5 miles in length.

Otherwise, continue from the col south-westwards, easily upwards to the last high top. This is Mynydd Craig-goch, the end of this long, westward-pointing ridge and four feet short of 2,000 feet high. From here a broad ridge drops to the south-east, towards the Vale of Pennant, but one can continue southwards for about three miles, over broken moorland to the little hill of 1,190 feet called Craig-y-garn directly overlooking the village of Llanfihangel-y-pennant. And so down to the rushing, chattering waters of the Afon Dwyfor. If the complete round is done, twelve summits are trodden and 16.5 miles covered.

Deserted Ramparts – Nantlle quarry with Craig Cwm Silin, behind

Chapter 13

ON THE RIDGES OF SNOWDON

Names and meanings – a note on the Snowdon Horseshoe.

Route A: Pen-y-Pass – Bwlch Moch – Cwm Glas – Bwlch Coch – Cwm Dyli – Pen-y-Pass.

Distance: 6 miles.

Grade: Strenuous

Starting Point: Pen-y-Pass (map reference: 648557)

Route B: Pen-y-Pass – Cwm Dyli – Gallt-y-Wenallt – Lliwedd -Bwlch-y-Saethau – Gribin Rib – Pen-y-Pass

Distance: 6 miles

Grade: Strenuous

Starting Point: Pen-y-Pass (map reference: 648557)

Maps: Ordnance Survey "Landranger" (1:50,000) Sheet 115 (Snowdon and Surrounding Area), Ordnance Survey "Outdoor Leisure" (1:25,000) Sheet 17 (Snowdonia – Snowdon and Conwy Valley Areas).

The name "Snowdon" requires some clarification for it is often used vaguely to mean a mountain, sometimes a whole mountain region.

"Eryri" is the original Welsh name given to the mountainous area we know today as Snowdonia. "Eryri" means "the abode of eagles" and was, presumably, a fitting title up to the late Middle Ages. "Snowdon" was the English counterpart of "Eryri", the name given to the mountain area of north-west Wales, and it was never the name for a single mountain or summit. It has been suggested that "Snowdon" was a title given by sailors as the latter would see snow lying in the high, north-facing gullies far into summer from their vessels in Conwy Bay or off Anglesey. It means literally "the mountains of snow".

Today "Snowdonia" is the region, "Snowdon" the massif containing four main (and numerous lesser) summits, and the highest of these – the "Snowdon" of popular acclaim – is properly called "Y Wyddfa". The late Sir John E. Lloyd explained why the highest summit was so named. In a charter granted to the Cistercian Abbey of Aberconwy in 1198 the summit was called "Wyddfa Fawr" – "the Great Tomb". Another name, "Carnedd y Cawr", upheld this idea for it means "the Giant's Cairn". The summit is, in fact, the traditional burial place of Rhita Gawr. This fierce giant was a king-killer of the first order, an ogre who dressed in a cloak made of king's beards. His greatest enemy was Arthur, who eventually slew Rhita Gawr and had a great cairn thrown over the giant upon the top of the highest summit of Eryri. Chapter 2 gives more detail of Arthur in Eryri but it is worth remembering that about 850 feet below this summit, upon Bwlch y Seathau to the south-east, is the traditional tomb of Arthur himself.

Llyn Llydaw from the summit of Crib Goch (3,023 ft)

And so Snowdon is a name best avoided but, if used, let is refer to the whole group of high summits forming a horseshoe about Llyn Llydaw and Llyn Glaslyn. The highest summit is Y Wyddfa, 3,560 feet above sea level and highest top south of the Scottish Highlands.

I am not going to detail some of the best-known scrambling or rambling routes on this massif. They are either too well-known or already so well described in various publications as to make restatement here unnecessary. The finest scramble in the whole region is the circuit of the famous Snowdon Horseshoe, from Pen-y-Pass, over the wonderful top of Crib Goch, on over Crib-y-Ddisgl and Y Wyddfa, and finally over Lliwedd and back to Pen-y-Pass. I have completed this circuit from Pen-y-Pass and back to Pen-y-Pass in 2 hours and 55 minutes, but on a day of deep snow and iced rocks it has taken 8 hours or more. Sometimes, in extreme winter conditions, the route is not practicable to any but a skilled ice climber. Conditions vary tremendously upon all mountains, and on the Snowdon Horseshoe conditions count for a lot, especially to the beginner or rambler of limited experience.

The north face of Lliwedd (2,947 ft) from Crib-y-Ddisgl (3,493 ft)

Route "A"

1. The first route I am going to suggest here is only about six miles on the map but this covers very steep terrain and requires plenty of time. It leaves Pen-y-Pass (map reference: 648557) and ascends the small, grass-covered hill which forms the traditional "First Nail in the Horseshoe". Upon the top of this hill one now follows the easy winding ridge that leads westwards to abut against the foot of Crib Goch's east ridge at the pass called Bwlch Moch, where the Pyg track goes over towards Lyn Llydaw. We are now at 1,925 feet and the next section of the ramble -into remote Cwm Glas – is reasonably level, though care is necessary to follow the correct line over the steepening ground ahead.

2. A bluff of rock is seen up under the scree, under Crib Goch's steep east ridge which leads from where we stand to the summit (3,023 feet). For about a quarter of an hour go up towards the summit and then notice a marshy flat below to the right. A small stream meanders through the marsh. Turn off to the right (north) here, the track is not very obvious as one proceeds. Up and down the little track goes, close beneath the steep, rocky flanks of the mountain's north ridge. Below are the cliffs towering over Cwm Beudy Mawr. I always think this path strongly reminiscent of the narrow path under the eastern flanks of the Mittaghorn between Plattjen and the Britannia Hut, with spectacular downward views to the Saastal, dominated by the snows of the Weissmies. The comparison is strengthened in early summer when purple saxifrage blooms in pretty clumps among occasional specimens of evergreen dwarf juniper growing prostrate against the rocks.

Cwm Glas Mawr

Eventually, the path breasts the smooth slope at the foot of Crib Goch's north ridge, and we can look across the wild hollow of Cwm Glas, "the big green hollow". It is one of the most dramatic mountain hollows in Britain, being overshadowed by great ridges and numerous cliffs which have become shrines to rock climbers. To Cwm Glas came the enigmatic Climbing Parson in the middle of the last century who endeavoured "to follow the sky-line of every mountain he visited". With him the walking or rambling era started in Snowdonia. After him is named the Parson's Nose, that famous piece of steep, dark rock which forms the base of the Clogwyn y Person arete (literally, "the cliff of the parson") at which we look across the width of Cwm Glas from our footpath's end below Crib Goch.

The Climbing Parson came first, it is recorded, to "his" Cliff by the path we have followed from Bwlch Moch, a path known today as the Goat Track.

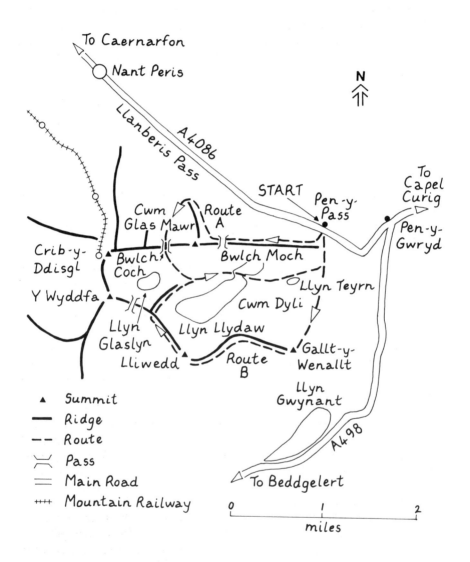

3. Now we cross the rough floor of the cwm to the little pool with its island. From here, from Llyn Glas, we can examine the fine rock architecture of Clogwyn y Person and the rest of the enclosing mountain walls. To the south is a low gap in the ridge between Crib Goch and Crib y-Ddisgl (3,493 feet). The summit of this latter, the second highest top in Snowdonia, is not visible from our viewpoint, but the sharp ridge ascending towards it is quite clear.

4. We are now going to cross the low gap ahead, to the right of the conspicuous Pinnacles of Crib Goch and to the left of the Clogwyn y Person arete. This is the 2,816 feet high Bwlch Coch, "the red pass". It provides a relatively easy route over to Cwm Dyli, the great hollow enclosed within the outstretched arms of the Snowdon Horseshoe.

The 1:50,000 map doesn't give much guidance now, for the broken ground and closeness of the contours does not help clarity. Once upon the 2,816 feet pass there is a clear view of the slope down into the great, dramatic hollow beyond when the clouds aren't low.

Here on Bwlch Coch one can see remains of the small enclosures erected in the summer of 1960 by the Nature Conservancy to study the effects upon the natural vegetation of partial and total exclusion of sheep grazing and to study the effect of the exclusion of sheep on vegetative recolonisation of eroded screes and to investigate the re-establishment of vegetation on eroded areas by artificial means. As one would expect at this altitude the changes have been only small so far, though there has been some return of grass species on enclosures which have been terraced and unterraced.

The use of fertilisers, the planting of turves and the use of straw mulching to provide additional stability are other things being studied here – and at other sites in Snowdonia – to see what effect they have upon regeneration of eroded grassland.

5. Down now to the south and at about 1,900 feet the well-worn Pyg Track is reached. By going left along this (towards the east) one soon reaches Bwlch Moch again and so down to Pen-y-Pass. Alternatively continue down the slope of Crib Goch to the shores of Llyn Llydaw near the ruins of the copper mine (map reference: 629546). By going along the wide track, the Miners' Track, back towards the east one has a level and

pleasant walk which takes one over the causeway across the narrow part of the lake near its north-eastern end. Many years ago the level of this lake was raised by the building of a dam across its outlet into lower Cwm Dyli so that water could be piped down to the power station at the head of the Vale of Gwynant. When the lake is full the causeway is covered and only in calm weather is it wise to wade over. Even then it can be dangerous as the water on either side is deep and I would never attempt a crossing of the flooded causeway in murky conditions or at night. It is far wiser to go around the head of the lake.

Mountain Railway

Bwlch Coch can be a bleak place when gale-force winds tear over the pass and soon lower one's body temperature. On a mild, summer's day it is a lovely spot, where the lakes on both sides beckon and the bellowings of locomotives on the Snowdon Mountain Railway sound distantly from beyond Crib y Ddisgl. Mention of the Snowdon Mountain Railway is perhaps a good place to recall the momentous opening of this line at Easter, 1896.

Hundreds of people gathered at Llanberis to see the first train leave for the summit of Y Wyddfa. The first train arrived at the summit at 12.15 p.m., where thick most covered the terminus. On arrival of the second train at the summit the first train set off on the descent, down into the mist. Soon after starting down the passengers felt a sharp jerk and then the train began to gather speed at an alarming rate! Very soon, however, the brakes on the carriage were applied and the passengers were able to get out, only to discover that their locomotive had disappeared!

Soon the driver and stoker appeared ascending out of the mist. The brakes on the engine had failed and, not being coupled to the carriage, the former had careered down the line. As it approached the wide bend above Clogwyn Station, the first station below the summit, the crew had jumped for their lives and the engine had left the lines and crashed down 400 feet in Cwm Glas Bach. For many years the twisted remains of this rack-and-pinion locomotive lay high up in Cwm Glas, overlooking Gwastadnant. Geoffrey Winthrop Young has recorded how he and his friends long treasured those brass relics brought down from the cwm.

Another facet of this incident concerns a young walker, new to the mountains, who was wandering in the mists of Cwm Glas Bach. Suddenly he was startled by the sight and sound of this locomotive falling out of the clouds. He fled from the mountains. We can imagine his feelings.

To the passengers of the first train another hazard presented itself in the form of the second train colliding with the stationary carriage of the first due to the dense cloud-cover. This was explained by the fact that the first locomotive had hit the telegraph poles alongside the line on its headlong journey, so breaking the overhead wires and giving the signal for the second train to leave the summit.

One of the passengers who jumped from the carriage of the first train before it stopped was the owner of a Llanberis hotel, he broke a leg and died the next morning following an operation. He was the only person to be seriously injured. Since that fateful opening run no accidents of any consequence to passengers have occurred on the Snowdon Railway.

Incidentally, the surface of the great hollow enclosed by the arms of the Snowdon Horseshoe has the doubtful honour of being the wettest place in Europe. Numerous rain-gauges have long recorded the annual precipitation in this great cwm. One such gauge on the southern slopes of Crib Goch recorded a total of 207 inches of precipitation in 1946, another recorded 198 inches in the same year where the infant Afon Glaslyn empties into Llyn Llydaw from Llyn Glaslyn towards the head of the cwm.

6. The Miners' Track winds on towards Pen-y-Pass, above the ruined miners' huts by the lovely little lake called Llyn Teyrn. A mile further on we get back to our starting point at Pen-y-Pass.

Route "B"

1. Another ramble over some less-popular terrain of the Snowdon massif starts from Pen-y-Pass and takes one along the Miners' Track as far as the big bend, where the track turns towards Llyn Teyrn. Leave the track here and go straight ahead, down into the wide open mouth of Cwm Dyli. Ahead, across the marshy Cwm's base, rises the "Last Nail in the Horseshoe", the great, swelling, green buttress of Gallt-y-Wenallt which drops steep and bold into Nant Gwynant. Geoffrey Winthrop Young considered this the "boldest brow in Europe". Looking at this great ridge-end from the road between Pen-y-Gwryd and Pen-y-Pass, especially on a day of sun and snow, the feeling of mighty power which that great scholar-mountaineer felt can be sensed. It is not a startling hill-shape, a Tryfan or a Lliwedd, but a profile of resignation and confidence.

2. Down into Cwm Dyli we go; notice the twin crags of the Teyrn Bluffs up to the right, fine bad-weather cliffs for novice and expert alike. There is a ruined cottage down here, a memory of the hard days in these hills when Cwm Dyli was far more remote than today. Down and over the pipe-line carrying water from Llyn Llydaw to the power-station below. Now up the first steepening of Gallt-y-Wenallt, by another ruined building, and in one thousand feet of ascent we reach the unpretentious, grassy top of the mountain 2,032 feet above sea level.

Remember that in this steep and sometimes difficult country a distance of six miles can take a long, long time. Although this particular route measures only six miles on the map it can take most of a day if time is allowed for looking at the wonderful mountain details on the way.

From this summit Crib Goch really looks like a "red ridge" in the sunlight, rising across the width of Cwm Dyli. Down on the bottom of the cwm are the drumlins, rounded mounds of boulder clay and glacial debris left by the great glacier which once occupied, and deepened, this hollow. Over to the right is the distant head of the lovely green Vale of Gwynant, but our route lies towards the sharp crest of Lliwedd.

3. On a day of sun and broken clouds driven by a westerly wind the atmosphere ahead is constantly changing as we go first over Lliwedd Bach (Little Lliwedd) and then rising up the mountain's east ridge, with ever-wider views down to Llyn Llydaw and across to the other side of the Horseshoe. Blue and silver light breaks in upon the crags and often the only sounds are of distant falling water and sheep bleatings.

In contrast to the steep, downward views to the north the southern flanks of Lliwedd are smoother, broken by boulders but bilberry covered and with few steep rock steps to hinder ascent or descent; however this slope down to the Vale of Gwynant is rarely trodden, save by shepherds.

4. The top of Lliwedd has two crowns, an eastern and a western summit. The highest point (2,947 feet) is a fine belvedere from which to view much of the eastern aspects of the Snowdon massif, and the distant line of Cardigan Bay to the south-west. Below us is the great precipice where rock climbing was so popular half a century and more ago, where Archer Thomson, George Leigh Mallory, Geoffrey Winthrop Young and others placed their criss-cross of long routes before lesser cliffs became popular. It is perhaps true to say that Lliwedd is today a neglected cliff, partly pensioned-off because, I fancy, it is rather too far to walk from the road for many modern cragsmen. What a commentary if this is true!

Y Wyddfa presents one of its finest aspects to us now, this view from the south-east reveals a powerful, pyramidal peak, a shapely mass with the long, supporting south-west ridge of Bwlch Main dropping off to the left above the smooth sweep of Cwm Tregalan. All this territory over which we look is charged with ancient history and the atmosphere is one of folk-lore of by-gone ages, the names of Arthur and Rhita Gawr sound in every hollow of weathered rocks.

5. Down now towards Y Wydffa, down the 500 feet to the pass between Lliwedd and the shoulder rising towards Y Wyddfa called Bwlch Ciliau "the pass of the hollows". One almost steps off Lliwedd's north-west ridge, onto the relatively level area of the pass, where a large cairn marks the point where the Watkin Path from Nant Gwynant comes up and turns along the ridge towards Y Wyddfa. We go along the broad and broken ridge, along the wide and eroded path which has become a veritable highway hewn from the mountain by the passage of thousands of feet in the last half century.

6. Care must now be taken to find the right place at which to turn off the ridge to the right (north-eastwards), especially in conditions of poor visibility. The ridge rises steadily towards the last pass before Y Wyddfa steepens ahead. This pass right beneath the highest summit is the famous Bwlch y Saethau, "the pass of the arrows", which connects the head of Cwm Dyli in the vicinity of Llyn Glaslyn with Cwm Tregalan.

7. Less than half a mile beyond the first pass – Bwlch Ciliau (map reference: 619537) – go over to the broken top of the ridge to the right and the broad, easy ridge of the Gribin will be seen leading down into Cwm Dyli, between little Llyn Glaslyn (source of the Afon Glaslyn and often green in colour on account of the presence of copper ores hereabouts) and the lower Llyn Llydaw.

8. At the foot of the Gribin ridge one crosses the rushing torrent of the young Afon Glaslyn and joins the Miners' Track where it swings down from the Britannia Copper Mines by Llyn Glaslyn towards Llyn Llydaw. If time allows it is interesting to go around the southern shore of the upper lake to see the old, wooden cross to the memory of a fallen climber. There is another cross, this time of marble, which stood beneath the great cliffs of Lliwedd to the memory of a climber who fell from one of the steep routes above. Unfortunately, vandals have smashed this white cross and I well remember years ago standing near its scattered remains directly below Lliwedd's shadowy northern face.

9. It is two and a half miles back to Pen-y-Pass now, down and along by the Miners' Track, over Llyn Llydaw's causeway and by Llyn Teyrn.

Alternatively, one can contour along the broken ground above Llyn Llydaw and gain the Pyg Track beneath Crib Goch's southern slopes at about 1,900 feet, go back over Bwlch Moch and so down the broad and broken track which is virtually a highway to Pen-y-Pass. A quieter, pleasanter way lies along the broad and grassy "First Nail in the Horseshoe" from Bwlch Moch, keeping high until it is simply a matter of running down the steep grass slopes into the car park at Pen-y-Pass.

Chapter 14

ALONG THE WATERSHED OF THE GLYDERS

Route: Capel Curig – Gallt yr Ogof – Nameless Peak – Glyder Fach – Glyder Fawr – Cwm Cneifio – Gwastadnant – Nant Peris, or Glyder Fawr – Esgair Felen – Beudy Mawr – Nant Peris

Distance: 9 miles.

Grade: Strenuous

Starting Point: Capel Curig (map reference: 721582)

Maps: Ordnance Survey "Landranger" (1:50,000) Sheet 115 (Snowdon and Surrounding Area); Ordnance Survey "Outdoor Leisure" (1:25,000) Sheet 17 (Snowdonia – Snowdon and Conwy Valley Areas).

There are two Glyders; the higher (western) summit rises to 3,279 feet and is logically Glyder Fawr ("the Big Glyder"), the lower (eastern) summit is 17 feet less and so is Glyder Fach ("the Little Glyder"). However, in the seventeenth century the massif was considered as one mountain, and the unique collection of huge boulders upon the summit of Glyder Fach was considered to be "the utmost top". The original name of Glyder means "a heap or pile" of stones and referred to the great quantity of piled rocks upon the summit ridge.

In the true tradition of the Northern Hemisphere this massif has a steep, cliffy northern face and an easier, smoother southern flank due to the extra erosion caused by the lingering ice upon the shaded, northern faces long ago – and today.

There are many routes for the rambler, some very popular, some rarely trodden. Cwm Idwal and the Devil's Kitchen are popular places, being easy to reach from the Holyhead road at Ogwen Cottage. The ascent of lovely Tryfan, "the three-headed summit", is a pilgrimage undertaken by thousands each year, the only Snowdonian mountain where scrambling is essential to reach the top (though Crib Goch could come into this class).

I shall describe just one route here, the fine ramble from Capel Curig to Nant Peris along the main watershed of the Glyders.

The east face of Tryfan (3,010 ft) seen from the London-Holyhead road, near Helyg

The Route

1. Behind Capel Curig post office (map reference: 721582) take the old road across the rushing waters of the Afon Llugwy and past Gelli Farm. Beyond this, go west, up the smooth-sided ridge of Cefn y Capel to the 1,509 feet top. Down to the south the twin Capel lakes of Llynau Mymbyr shine on sunlit days, backed by the sombre slopes of Moel Siabod.

2. The ridge dips slightly as we turn towards the north-west and ascend about one thousand feet more to the rocky ridge which becomes the summit of the first principal hill of the massif, Gallt yr Ogof ("the slope of the cave"). It commands the top of the ridge which slants up from the broad valley separating the Glyders and the Carneddau, drained by the Afon Llugwy. Below, to the north-east, is the hollow of Nant y Gors overshadowed by the crags of Gallt yr Ogof where numerous relatively unpopular climbing routes are to be found.

Far down the southern slopes of the mountain is the mountain farm of Dyffryn Mymbyr where Thomas Firbank lived before World War II and about which he wrote the best-seller *I Bought a Mountain*. Esme still lives at and farms Dyffryn Mymbyr and its land extends up to the watershed of the Glyders, our route from Capel Curig and on towards Nant Peris.

3. In less than a mile the higher summit of the Nameless Peak is gained, a smooth mountain-top of 2,636 feet a little to the east of the narrow lake of Llyn Caseg-fraith – "the lake of the piebald mare". Here the water stands in many pools and on days of bright sunshine and floating clouds it is easy to imagine a mountain pony peering into the lake's surface and imagining the cloud shadows to be piebald markings. To avoid wet feet on this ill-drained and level ridge-top care should be taken between the scattered pools.

4. The lovely profile of Tryfan's triple crown comes nearer and alters shape, an unusual viewpoint for this well-known and well-loved mountain. Here we see it above the rocky shelves of Cwm Tryfan, a rocky and broken cwm-floor, even for Snowdonia. The old track between Pen-y-Gwryd and Ogwen Cottage (used by copper miners and quarry-men) is crossed soon after Llyn Caseg-fraith and now begins the 800 feet ascent to one of Britain's most unusual summits, that of Glyder Fach.

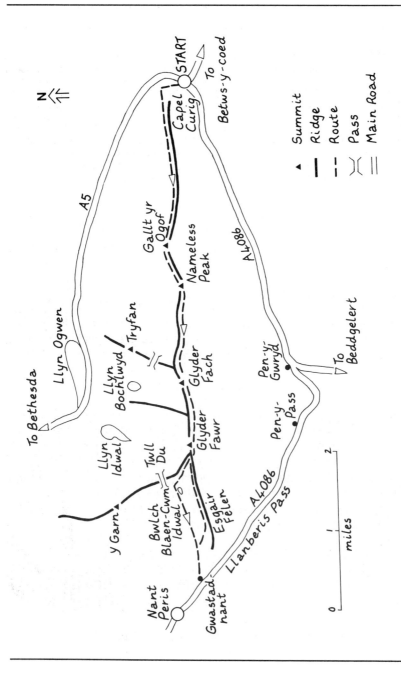

Glyder Fach

On a misty day, on a day of moving vapours and silence, the great, strewn, grey slabs and blocks can indeed seem weird. The great Cantilever near the topmost pile of rocks lies apparently balanced upon other blocks and often I've walked out to its farthest end, half expecting to over balance. Despite the great gatherings of people at its outer end the cantilever still stands as it did when Pennant toured Wales in 1780. He climbed the Glyders at the first opportunity and remarked that the summit of Glyder Fach "was covered with groups of columnar stones, of vast size, from ten to thirty feet long, lying in all directions . . . One was about twenty-five feet long and six broad; I climbed up, and on stamping it with my foot felt a strong tremulous motion from end to end."

Herbert R. C. Carr has written that it is hard to believe that Glyder Fach is 17 feet lower than Glyder Fawr and states that "the Fach always looks the monarch of the group".

The Cantilever Rock near the summit of Glyder Fach

5. And so from this most unusual top we go again westwards, down and over (or round on the southern side) the shapely sub-summit called Castell-y-Gwynt, "the Castle of the Winds". What a fine point is is, a tower or pyramid looking out over the wide pass of Bwlch-y-Ddwy-Glyder (the pass of the two Glyders) and over the sloping Gribin ridge to the distant Nant Ffrancon in the north.

6. On again and so, stepping onto the slopes of the higher Glyder a change in the terrain is noticeable; smooth, grassy slopes extend towards the west, a change in the floral pattern caused by the alkaline nature of the rocks here, dolerite rocks with a high calcium carbonate content, compared with the acid lava rocks supporting heather and bilberry upon Glyder Fach's topmost slopes.

The Gribin ridge descends northwards towards Llyn Idwal, a rock-and-grass ridge which supports a rich pattern of flora near its base above the lake, on an outcrop of calcareous tuffs. A notable plant found here is the rare Mountain Avens (*Dryas octopetala*), its white petals somewhat reminiscent of the lovely cloudberry of Pennine moors. This site is one of only two in Snowdonia where this species is known to grow. Beyond the Gribin ridge-top we can look down upon the steep-sided Cwm Cneifion (the nameless Cwm), overlooked by the great profile of Clogwyn Du – the aptly named "Black Cliff". Over the top of this cliff the Senior's Ridge descends towards Idwal, and soon we are upon the open, rock-spiked top of Glyder Fawr.

7. A wonderful vista can be enjoyed on clear days, over mountains and valleys to far, blue haze over the sea. Snowdon's many tops to the south-west and the high, swelling brows of the Carneddau to the north-east. From here it is possible to go down to the north, making for the square little lake at 2,325 feet called Llyn y Cwn, "the lake of the dogs", so called due to the traditional hunting of deer hereabouts in ancient times. The lake was always supposed to contain monocular fish – "eel, trout and perch, all of which have only one eye, the left being wanting". A short distance over to the north-east is the top of Twll Du, the Devil's Kitchen, with the famous view downwards to Llyn Idwal.

8. From Llyn y Cwn turn down Cwm Cneifio and so by the fast-falling Afon Lâs to the steep-tilted fields above Gwastadnant and the road a mile above Nant Peris.

8a. Alternatively, one can take the long, south-west pointing ridge from the top of Glyder Fawr. This is the high crest seen to advantage from Llanberis Pass and called Esgair Felen. It can be a wild and arctic place in the depth of winter, blasted by icy winds which grip and solidify the scree. At the lower end of the ridge the big, loose cliff called Craig Nant Peris drops towards Llanberis Pass, two thousand feet below.

Thunderstorm on Snowdon from near the summit of Glyder Fawr

Craig Nant Peris

It is a wonderful situation, almost Alpine in scale; and from the top of the cliff in summer one can look across the void of the pass to the smoky eruptions on the Llechog ridge of Snowdon and above Cwm Glas Bach made by the locomotives on the Snowdon Railway.

The first route climbed on Craig Nant Peris was up the South-West Arete, by G. W. H. Tunzelmian in March 1893. Forty-two years later C. H. S. R. Palmer and a friend made the other five best routes here, the best probably being Central Buttress Arete. The others lie between these two first routes and consist of two gullies called Tweedledum and Tweedledee with a small buttress between them called, appropriately, The Rattle!

As we look down from the top of the Central Buttress there is an easy gully to our left (east). This can be descended relatively easily and gives 2,000 feet of scrambling down to Llanberis Pass. It is Bryant's Gully, the longest route in Snowdonia, and probably the longest south of the Highlands. Its ascent makes an interesting scramble in summer and a serious expedition in winter conditions. *It should not be attempted by the inexperienced mountaineer.*

9a. Our route now lies down the long and grassy slopes, with scattered scree and rocks, towards the fields above Gwastadnant, where the Afon Lâs joins the Afon Nant Peris in the bottom of the valley. On the way down there are many level places where, if it is warm and dry, we can sit and watch the late sun descending towards the Irish Sea. I know of fewer pleasanter spots to ponder for a while after the exertions of the day upon the cliffs of the northern flanks of the Glyders or on our walk from the far end of the massif. There is a particularly sunny belvedere just below the top of Craig Nant Peris, and another much lower down by a steep, rocky corner draped in ivy.

10a. Eventually the path is reached which drops from the col between Glyder Fawr and Y Garn, near the Devil's Kitchen. This is the well-worn and often-used track over the watershed between Cwm Idwal and Nant Peris, a path which has been used by generations of ramblers and climbers. Twenty five or so years ago this right of way was suddenly disputed by the farmer at Gwastadnant. The then Caernarfonshire County Council claimed it was a right of way and the farmer eventually accepted it as such. We go down by the Afon Lâs and out onto the main road close by Gwastadnant, less than a mile above Nant Peris.

*Summer on Craig Nant Peris, looking across Llanberis Pass to Snowdon's
Llechog Ridge*

Chapter 15

THE CARNEDDAU

Route: Llyn Ogwen – Cwm Lloer – Pen yr Oleuwen – Carnedd Dafydd – Carnedd Llewelyn – Yr Elen – Carnedd Llewelyn – Pen yr Helgi-du -Pen Llithrig-y-Wrach – Capel Curig

Distance: 11.5 miles.

Grade: Very Strenuous

Starting Point: East end of Llyn Ogwen (map reference: 666605)

Maps: Ordnance Survey "Landranger" (1:50,000) Sheet 115 (Snowdon and Surrounding Area);Ordnance Survey "Outdoor Leisure" (1:25,000) Sheet 17 (Snowdonia – Snowdon and Conwy Valley Areas).

If the ridges of the Snowdon massif are sharp and angular and the Glyders are characterised by their broken, boulder-piled tops and cwms, the great massif to the north of the Ogwen Valley is one of wide, elevated and sweeping shoulders – the most extensive mountain group of Snowdonia, broad and high and lonely. There is twice as much land over 2,000 feet here as upon the Glyders, and four times as much as upon the Snowdon massif.

One can walk upon the smooth ridges of the Carneddau day-in and day-out and see few other humans, possibly no one if you know when and where to go. Here stand two of the highest summits in North Wales – Carnedd Llewelyn (3,484 feet) and Carnedd Dafydd (3,426 feet) the third and fourth highest mountain-tops respectively, coming after Y Wyddfa and Crib y Ddisgl.

It is not surprising to find that a poem of divination, or "cywydd brud", attributed to the fifteenth-century bard Rhys Goch of Eryri refers to the highest Carnedd by its modern name for it was probably so called after Llewelyn the Great (1194-1240), the great Welsh prince who lived at Aber on the north coast and had an observation post on this mountain. It is recorded that upon the summit stood a fortified "carnedd" but this had been ruined beyond recognition as early as 1847. Carnedd Dafydd is lower than its neighbour by 58 feet and possesses upon its summit ridge at least three cairns, or stone structures. Were they burial chambers or fortifications? Dafydd, after whom this mountain seems to be named, was the brother of the last Welsh prince, Llewelyn ap Gruffydd.

As on the high gritstone moorlands of the Peak District few trees are found here, though there is evidence that birch covered much of the surface up to quite high elevations in pre-historic times – birch stumps can still be found in the peat up to nearly 2,000 feet as on Bleaklow in Peakland. Besides the change in climate, felling and the activities of grazing animals have denuded the Carneddau of their woodland and these animals (sheep today) prevent re-colonisation.

Sundew, Bog Asphodel and Cotton Sedge are the plants which dominate the ill-drained hollows, together with Bog Rush. Grass, notably Mat Grass and Sheep's Fescue, is the dominant plant type, not bilberry and heather. In this respect the Carneddau can be likened to Bleaklow rather than the plateau of Kinder Scout in the Peak District. Unlike those latter areas the Carneddau has large areas with an elevation up to almost 3,500 feet so that the upper thousand feet exhibit a fine example (the best in the whole of Wales) of the arctic-tundra habitat found especially in the Cairngorms.

Wheatears are relatively common birds of these wild and open mountain-sides, as is the Ring Ouzel. Mountain ponies which have become wild and bred over the generations can be seen in small herds at the grassy head of some remote valleys, as in Cwm Pen-llafar. The fine coats of these animals lend colour to these uplands, reminding me of the ponies found grazing on the moorlands of Rhum in the Hebrides.

Strengthening the similarity to Bleaklow is the fact that if one is extremely lucky a glimpse may be had of a mountain hare, introduced here in 1880 by Lord Penrhyn. Though they established themselves I have never seen one here, and there have been few records of them having been seen in recent years. In certain lights the crests of the Carneddau appear like arctic deserts, but the wild goats which are sometimes seen on them dispel the illusion and bring one back to the reality that one is in wildest North Wales. These goats, usually led by an old and bearded billie with beard of chocolate shade, can often be discovered on the Glyders or high above Nant Gwynant on Gallt-y-Wenallt. Once, I recall, we came across a little kid among the ash trees at the foot of Clogwyn y Bustach (the cliff overlooking upper Nant Gwynant where Lockwood's well-loved Chimney rears) on a cold February day. Its parents had moved off in search of grazing and, for a time, the kid bleated plaintively, and ran after us hoping to find the nanny where we went.

Once we watched a stranded goat upon one of the steep cliffs that drop to Llanberis Pass. For days it stayed upon its ledge, then, when all vegetation within reach had been devoured, it disappeared as mysteriously as it had come. In winter the goats descent to the lowland and are a pest to the gardeners of Nant Peris. The late Ina Lynas Smith of Coed Gwydr had a long running battle with the trespassing Glyder goats each winter. They seemed able to get past the tallest fencing and wire netting – the colder the weather the bolder they became. The most likely place to see goats on the Carneddau is on the rocky slopes of Pen-yr-Oleu-wen, above the shallow waters of Llyn Ogwen. And so to the route of the ramble over these hills.

Pen-yr-Oleu-wen (3,210 ft) from the path to Carnedd Dafydd

The bold profile of Pen-yr-Oleu-wen, "the hill of the white light", rears immediately to the north of Llyn Ogwen, hemming in the northern side of the Ogwen Valley. It is the third highest mountain of the Carneddau, its broad top reaching 3,210 feet above sea level. There are two normal ways up to the top from Ogwen, the broken south-western ridge and the eastern ridge.

For this ramble I shall describe briefly the way up by the eastern ridge, though some readers may prefer the steadily steep and rocky route up the other side, direct from Pont Pen-y-benglog (map reference: 649605) at the outflow from Llyn Ogwen.

Yr Elen (3,151 ft) from the top of Ysgolion Duon

The Route

1. At the eastern end of the lake leave the A5 road and walk northwards along the track past Glan Dena (the hut belonging to the Midland Association of Mountaineers) overlooking the level and ill-drained delta of the Afon Dena at the head of the lake. The old Holyhead road went this way, then along the northern shore and down the western side of the Nant Ffrancon pass. Soon the farm of Tal-y-llyn-Ogwen is passed and we ascend the easy slopes to the north for almost a mile, keeping close by the Afon Lloer up to Cwm Lloer.

Cwm Lloer

In fine weather this is a grand walk; in summer, bog asphodel blooms amongst the rough grasses and butterwort peeps near mossy hollows. Suddenly the slope levels out and we enter the surprising mountain hollow called Cwm Lloer. It is a basin hemmed in on three sides by very steep slopes of between one thousand and one thousand three hundred feet. The steep and broken ground of Clogwyn Mawr overlooks the cwm on the east, and occupying its floor is the little lake of Ffynnon Lloer at approximately 2,100 feet above sea level. On a sunny day one can sit and watch the silent lake reflecting the brown slopes and dark shadows around and, as often as not, there is an angler hoping for a bite by the 3-4 ounce trout which live here. The outflow from this lovely lake is over polished slabs. The name Lloer requires some explanation for it means "the moon" – Cwm Lloer is "the Hollow of the Moon" and Ffynnon Lloer is "the Spring of the Moon". There may well be some connection between these names and Pen-yr-Oleu-wen for "the hill of the white light" overlooks both "the Spring" and "the Hollow of the Moon". The lunar reference probably lingers as a relic of astronomical observances, when it was considered wise to look for the first appearance of the new moon each month from a high vantage point. Maybe the inhabitants of this region, especially the druids and bards, came up into this cwm to have a first, and lucky, glimpse of the rising new moon.

2. From here there is a direct scramble westwards to the top of Pen yr Oleu-wen up the east ridge. The 1,100 feet takes an hour or so if the pace is not forced and full advantage is taken of the views on either side. Beyond the summit the ridge swings round above Cwm Lloer, past the two prehistoric cairns marked on the O.S. map. The smooth, grassy slopes are crossed before the 3,426 feet top of Carnedd Dafydd. Beyond this top there are good views down to the north, into the head of Cwm Llafar; the long hollow drained by the Afon Llafar, fed by the numerous streams which gurgle off the northern slopes of Carnedd Dafydd and the western slopes of Carnedd Llewelyn. It has been suggested that the name Llafar ("a voice") refers to the noise in this great hollow of the many falling waters.

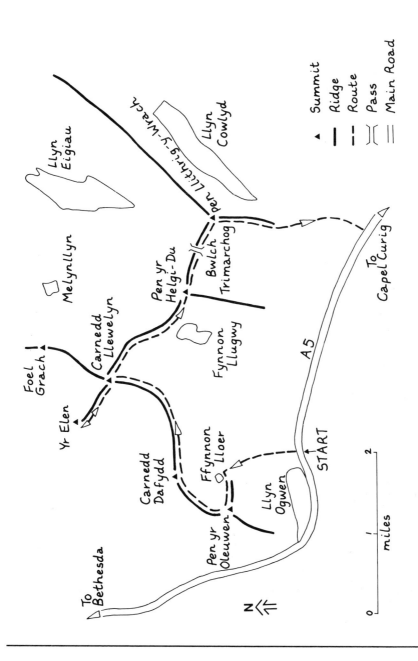

Llyn Eigiau

Llyn Cowlyd

Llechtyd-y-Wrach

Melynllyn

Foel Grach

Carnedd Llewelyn

Pen yr Helgi-Du

Bwlch Trimarchog

Yr Elen

Fynnon Lluguy

Carnedd Dafydd

Ffynnon Lloer

Pen yr Oleuwen

Llyn Ogwen

START

A5

To Capel Curig

To Bethesda

N

miles

0   1   2

▲ Summit
| Ridge
┆ Route
)(Pass
= Main Road

3. Out of sight from our ridge-top route here the great, vegetated cliff of Ysgolion Duon ("the Black Ladders") drops into the cwm, a cliff with many notable climbing routes, notably the 900 feet of Western Gully, first ascended in 1901. Continuing along the undulating ridge for another mile we soon go up the gentle slopes to the top of the highest Carnedd, the third highest point in North Wales.

4. Away to the north the smooth domes and ridges of the range sweep on like mid-Asian upland towards Aber and the north coast. Our route now drops down to the west for a short way, along the stony spur leading out to the isolated 3,151 feet top of Yr Elen, "the hill of the fawn". (Not covered on sheet 17 of the 1:25,000 scale map). From this outlier there are lovely views to the west and Elidir Fawr takes on a most unusual profile, that of a pure cone, a distant pyramid rising beyond the Carnedd y Filiast – Foel Goch ridge and this side of the western sea. Steeply below to the north is the tiny lake of Ffynnon Caseg, "the mare's lake", in its dark and secret hollow and out of which runs the stream which becomes Afon Caseg.

Deep lake of the Carneddau – Craig Dulyn seen across Llyn Dulyn from near its outlet

Craig yr Ysfa

At one point it is worth stopping to look down into the space below known as the Amphitheatre, a hollow bounded by great cliffs with bilberry and heather ledges. Across upon the Amphitheatre Wall the Pinnacle can be picked out high upon the face, the main feature on this wall and the route up it is called Pinnacle Wall which was first climbed by the great Colin Kirkus, alone on a June day in 1931. I have often arrived at this level viewpoint after completing a route on the part of Craig yr Ysfa which lies directly below. I have groped up in pitch darkness when snow and ice clothed the rocks after a long and slow ascent of Amphitheatre Buttress with a large party, to be met by a freezing wind blowing off the tops of the Carneddau, and I have arrived after a quick summer climb when we lay here in the burning sunlight watching isolated cloud-shadows slant leisurely across the hillsides.

5. Return now along the ridge to the summit of Carnedd Llewelyn and go down the east ridge, making for the arete leading to the next summit of 2,732 feet, called Pen yr Helgi-du. In less than a mile of easy descent we are passing the top of the great cliff called Craig yr Ysfa, "the crag of the sheepwalk".

6. Now on down and onto the level arete separating Cwm Eigiau with its lake and lonely sheep-walks from the hollow to the south containing Ffynnon Llugwy, "the well of clear water". It is, maybe, surprising to realise that Llyn Eigiau stands over 560 feet lower than Ffynnon Llugwy.

7. Soon we reach the point where the arete abuts against the shoulder of Pen yr Helgi-du. The ascent begins suddenly, for a short distance to the 2,732 foot summit of "the hill of the black hound". At the point where the arete joins the shoulder (map reference: 712626) there is a relatively level traversing track southwards which is a quick way down to the Holyhead road near Helyg. It soon joins the smooth and grassy ridge of Y Braich, by which feature progress is rapid.

8. The last summit of our ramble is well seen in clear conditions from the top of Pen yr Helgi-du for it is only one and a half miles distant as the crow flies across the graceful pass between. Go straight down to this low point on the watershed, Bwlch Trimarchog – the Pass of the Three Horsemen -which is 662 feet below the last top. At the bottom of the slope below this pass, on the southern side, a marker stone stood to mark the spot where three parish boundaries join. Tradition states that three riders, one from each parish presumably, met annually on the pass to settle any matters concerning their territories. Another supposition states that the name of the place is derived from the fact that a group of

broken, upstanding rocks can be seen from the northern side, from Cwm Eigiau, and these silhouettes appear to sit astride the ridge. Whichever is the true reason we can be sure that the name of the pass is very ancient.

9. Another 550 feet of ascent brings us to the conical top of Pen Llithrig-y-wrach. Here is a fine hill, exhibiting a bold profile of apparently immense height when seen from Capel Curig. The eastern face drops steeply down to the deep waters of Llyn Cowlyd and facing over to the crags of Creigiau Gleision.

This long lake (really a reservoir) is very deep – probably the deepest in Snowdonia – and dangerous. In its waters are brown trout and Loch Leven trout which grow to a good size and, according to that great authority, the late Arthur Lockwood of Pen-y-Gwryd, are free risers and best on August evenings when there is a stiff breeze blowing.

I remember a late December night years ago when we set out from Tal-y-waen, hospitable house of the late George Dwyer and family, and rushed up over the wet moor and onto the mountain's southern ridge. It was a very dark night and we were thankful for the smattering of snow that dusted the upper slopes. On the summit the black clouds suddenly parted and the moon shone across to light the high summits and the edges of the clouds turned to silver. Our descent was made more easy by the convenient cloud-breaks and shafts of moonlight.

10. We go down that same south ridge towards Capel Curig, crossing the leat which carries water from the heads of numerous south-flowing streams like the Afon Llugwy round the slopes and so into Llyn Cowlyd to give a greater "head" of water there. If one looks carefully one of the footbridges crossing the leat will be found – constructed really for driving sheep across – or alternatively it is usually possible to jump across the channel and so proceed down the slope. The path passing close by Tal-y-waen (map reference: 717594) is shown on the map and soon the Holyhead road is gained and it is only a mile down into Capel Curig, or four miles back to the starting point by Llyn Ogwen.

Chapter 16

THE ELIDIRS AND THE MARCHLYN LAKES

Route: Nant Peris – Elidir Fawr – Elidir Fach – Marchlyn Bach – Marchlyn Mawr – Carnedd y Filiast – Mynydd Perfedd – Foel Goch – Y Garn -Twll Du – Gwastadnant – Nant Peris

Distance: 10 miles.

Grade: Very Strenuous

Starting Point: Nant Peris (map reference: 605585)

Maps: Ordnance Survey "Landranger" (1:1:50,000) Sheet 115 (Snowdon and Surrounding Area); Ordnance Survey "Outdoor Leisure" (1:25,000) Sheet 17 (Snowdonia – Snowdon and Conwy Valley Areas).

Nant Peris is really Old Llanberis, the ancient settlement at the northern foot of the Pass of Llanberis. It is a sheltered little village with wonderful views of the steep mountains all about and there are numerous well-sited trees to act as attractive foregrounds. Until a few years ago the place was relatively unspoilt, but I am afraid that the general increase in popularity of the hills of late has spoilt some of this charm, especially at holiday times. Even thirty years ago Nant Peris was relatively unspoilt. Today we must go during the middle of the week, and out of the holiday season, to savour the original charm of the village and its environs.

Nant Peris gets its name from Saint Peris, a sixth-century Celtic holy man who came to this wild valley and based himself near a well which can still be seen a short distance to the east of the church and called Ffynnon Peris Sant. It stands in the garden of an old cottage which is shaded by a most peculiarly shaped larch tree and called Tynyffynnon. In olden times the well attracted many cripples and diseased persons who looked here for a cure. In the well there are always two fish, the appearance of which foretells that a cure is likely. The cell of Saint Peris was located near the present old church, a low structure of twelfth-century origin with fifteenth and seventeenth century additions. The fastigiate Irish yews in the graveyard set the old building off wonderfully against the bold background of steep slopes around.

It is surprising to learn that the only way up to Nant Peris until one hundred and seventy years ago was by boat from Cwm-y-glo below Llyn Padarn. All heavy goods and provisions were rowed up the twin lakes – Llyn Padarn and Llyn Peris – and then carried up the short distance to Nant Peris. Margaret ferch Evan lived at Pen-y-llyn ("the lower end of Llyn Padarn") during the eighteenth century, and was famed for her skill as a boat-builder, oarswoman and hunter. Overlooking the lower end of Llyn Peris are the ruins of Dolbadarn Castle, a native Welsh structure which was for twenty years the prison of Owen Goch, Llewelyn's brother. The thirteenth-century tower still stands boldly above the lake, the only part still standing of what is believed to have been a fortress built by the Welsh about 1250 which became defunct after Edward I had overrun North Wales. It is of the same type as the castle of Dolwyddelan in the Lledr valley to the south-east of Moel Siabod. This latter fortress stands in a powerful position high above the Afon Lledr, the twelfth-century keep now restored. Dolwyddelan Castle is thought to have been the birthplace of Llewelyn the Great and is one of the oldest masonry fortresses in North Wales.

The road goes up towards the confines of the Pass of Llanberis from Nant Peris and just where the slopes close in stand the scattered cottages and farmsteads centred on Gwastadnant (map reference: 613577).

A short distance below Gwastadnant is the cottage called Coed Gwydr of fond memory. This was the home of Ina Lynas Smith from 1922 to her death in 1990; she is remembered by many mountaineers for hospitality extended through the years. Quiet summer evenings in the picturesque hillside garden are remembered alongside her splendid catering; and conversations ranging from the habits of herons and routes in hidden cwms to watercolour techniques and the old gentry of Anglesey or Lleyn.

The Route

1. From Nant Peris we take the path almost opposite the old church and go up by the tumbling waters of the little Afon Gafr towards the 1,100 feet contour and then traverse towards the north and so into the lower end of the wide, straight valley drained by the Afon Dudodyn. Up there rises one of the largest mountain-sides south of the Highlands, the south-east flank of Elidir Fawr rising wide, smooth and almost unbroken to the summit ridge and the top at 3,029 feet above sea level.

The old name for this beautiful mountain was Carnedd Elidyr, believed to commemorate Elidyr Mwynfawr who was the husband of the daughter of the Welsh chieftain Maelgwn Gwynedd. E. W. Steeple records the tradition that Elidyr Mwynfawr arrived in North Wales on a fine horse which carried a load of seven and a half persons, the half being Elidyr's jester who ran at the horse's side and held onto the leather crupper extending from the saddle to the tail!

2. From the Afon Dudodyn there is now a 1,929 feet ascent ahead to the top of the higher Elidir – almost 2,700 feet from the road at Nant Peris. I always relish this long uphill walk, really an easy ascent over alternating dry grasses, rushes and scattered boulders. Only near the top, when the slopes of the summit ridge are reached does the extensive area of exposed rock change from the easy things below. Often have I come up this long mountain-side in the hot sunshine of a summer morning to be met by a chilling wind blowing onto the north-western side, off Anglesey and the far-away sea.

Ring ouzels fly about here and the wide valley of the Dudodyn echoes with the call of the cuckoo in early summer. Away to the north-east the Carneddau dominate the skyline that way, and the Snowdon massif rises to the south with the tiny track of the Mountain Railway winding upwards.

Elidir Fawr has an axis running from south-west to north-east and at the former end, the ridge-end overlooking Llyn Padarn and Llyn Peris, the great Dinorwig quarries have slowly taken out a massive piece of the mountain. The larger part is composed of Cambrian slate which has been formed by the compression of a thick mass of purple shale which was

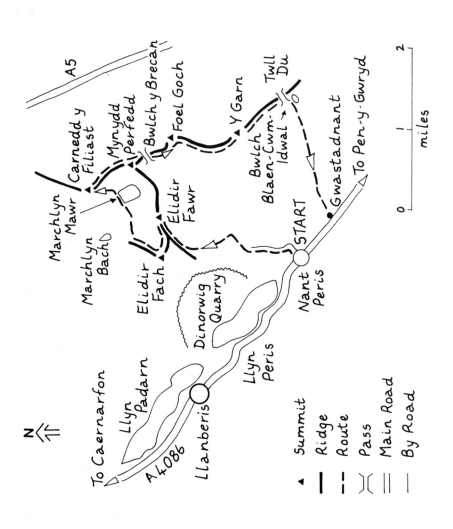

laid down in marine conditions as shown by the fossils found today in the rocks of this particular series; in fact, the oldest known fossils of Snowdonia have been found in the green mudstones above the purple shale here.

Slowly, then, Elidir Fawr has been eaten away by the activities of man, from both the Llanberis and the Bethesda sides. The highest quarry workings reach the 2,000 feet contour on the south-western side.

An Ancient Land

The view down to Llanberis and Llyn Padarn from the top of Elidir Fawr leads the eye away down the Seiont Valley and the distant levels of Anglesey with the thin line of the Menai Straits cutting across the vista in the middle distance. We are looking down and out of Snowdonia proper, from ancient rocks to even more ancient rocks. Forming "the pale rugged hills around the outer end of Llyn Padarn" is the ancient Padarn Ridge which stretches for thirteen miles between Bethesda and the village of Llanllyfni. It is only a "ridge" in the geological sense, a band of Pre-Cambrian rock (the oldest known material of the earth) which consists of pale-coloured rocks which originated largely as glassy lava sheets from volcanic eruption. Much of this material has become devitrified to produce the present-day pale, hard rock well seen in the smooth outcrops enclosing the lower end of Llyn Padarn. This, then, is the best exposure on the mainland of North Wales of the oldest rock upon which subsequent formations were erected, to give rise to the mountains of the region. There is, by the way, a similar, though shorter, ridge of pre-Cambrian rock running between Bangor and Caernarfon overlooking the Menai Straits.

In clear weather I know of no better place from which to examine this wide sweep of ancient territory stretching Anglesey-wards than the tops of Elidir Fawr and Elidir Fach.

---

3. Make down to the north, then towards the west, a steep slope of scree and stones leading to the flat and tundra-like shoulder marking the top of the mountain's lesser brother, Elidir Fach, at 2,964 feet.

4. Going down the smooth north ridge of the lesser summit we now make for the lovely lake of Marchlyn Bach, 1,557 feet above sea level. Cradled in a small, north-facing hollow this was a little visited lake, part of the all-embracing Vaynol Estate – the once major landowners of the district between the high mountains and the Menai Straits. Vaynol Park and Hall lie overlooking the Menai Straits close to Port Dinorwig, the place from whence slates were shipped overseas after the journey on the private quarry railway from the quarries upon Elidir.

5. Go round now to the eastern bank of the larger lake and go up the steep slope towards the summit of Carnedd y Filiast (2,694 feet). From

The Marchlyn Lakes

Marchlyn Bach gets little sun in wintertime, but on a hot and sunny morning in early June I came down to the silent, glassy water's edge and stripped for a plunge. The water was not unduly cold as I splashed about but suddenly there was a blinding flash and an explosion at the lower end of the lake. A thunderstorm had quickly gathered of which I was unaware, and the light faded from the sky all about, the hollow went dark as I climbed from the water and dressed. It did not rain and soon the thunder died away and the sun came forth again, but conditions were now unsettled so I made all speed for the upper, and larger lake.

The upper lake is Marchlyn Mawr, about half a mile distant from and 422 feet higher than the smaller one. It has been transformed in the recent past. It has been artificially deepened by a huge, curving impounding wall to act as the upper reservoir of the Dinorwig pump storage hydro-electricity scheme, hidden from sight deep inside Elidir Fawr. The level of water in Marchlyn Mawr rises and falls depending on the time of day. The lake is shaded on three sides by the steep mountain slopes, especially on the south-western side where the cliffs of Craig Cwrwgl – the Pillar of Elidir – rise darkly. This "pillar" is the most isolated peak in the whole of Wales, in fact, it is the only one which requires more than a few feet of rock climbing to get to the top. The best known route upon the cliff is Corrugated Cracks, a 160 feet high climb of severe standard first ascended in July 1937. The lake below this lonely cliff was almost circular even before the impounding wall was constructed. It is seen to advantage from the narrow ridge between Mynydd Perfedd and Elidir Fawr (map reference: 617615).

the top of this true hill-end of the Glyder main watershed, a ridge which runs right round from Capel Curig and descends from this high viewpoint now reached to the north, to the complicated workings of the Penrhyn Slate Quarries above Bethesda, we feel at the "end" of a range or ridge with wide spaces on three sides, especially to the east where steep rocks fall into the steep-floored hollow of Cwm Graianog, "the gravelly hollow". The slabs forming the cliffs lie at a relatively easy angle and are eroded to produce a unique climbing ground of shallow grooves and parallel slabs.

The name of this mountain means, literally, "the cairn of the female greyhound" and presumably owes its title to the miliast (a female greyhound) which was a symbol of Ceridwen, the Welsh mythological goddess of Nature. There is a 2,194 feet high hill four miles north-east of Arenig Fach also called Carnedd y Filiast and there are other places in North Wales with the word "Filiast" in their name so that it seems likely that this goddess was widely known and revered in prehistoric times. Turn to the south from the triangulation station on the summit and in a mile of level going the top of Mynydd Perfedd is reached, a stony level with a tumbled stone enclosure at 2,664 feet. This hill really forms the joining of three ridges, the one descending from Elidir Fawr, the level one reaching out the way we have just walked, and the third sweeping on towards the main massif of the Glyders, hence its name which means "the centre mountain".

Spring snow – looking north-east to Elidir Fawr and Y Garn (right) from near the summit of Y Wyddfa

6. The way ahead is straightforward, down to the col of Bwlch y Brecan with its fine view down the wide, straight valley of the Dudodyn – crossed and noticed earlier in the day when we ascended from Nant Peris and now seen from its very head, on the watershed where Welsh Mountain sheep invariably graze in all but the worst of weathers.

7. When the top of Foel Goch is reached there is a wonderfully airy view down the mountain's east ridge, down into Cwm Goch and the meandering Afon Ogwen in the wide flood-plain of the Nant Ffrancon over 2,000 feet below. Southwards again, along and down and up onto the last, and highest, summit of the day, dominating the whole complex of Ogwen. This is Y Garn, "The Rock", a bulky peak of fine lines and boldly plunging ridges on the eastern side, contrasting with the expansive, unbroken western flanks above Nant Peris. Here we stand at 3,104 feet and survey Llyn Ogwen, Tryfan's shattered western face and the shadowed northern cliffs of the Glyders. Directly below our summit

is the hanging valley of Cwm Clyd, "the sheltered hollow", held between the parallel east ridges of the mountain. Little Llyn Clyd is a favourite spot of mine, a quiet place to camp and watch the first rays of the rising sun catch the topmost slopes of Y Garn. The steep, shaley slopes between lake and summit are treacherous in summer but make a fine mountaineering route in winter when held in the grip of frozen snow.

Choughs and Ravens

Choughs fly about the shadowed rocks of rearing Foel Goch ahead of us. These sombre members of the crow family have red bills and legs and their normal calls are "kyow" and "k'chuff" as they fly buoyantly beneath a dark crest or falling bilberry crag, sometimes exhibiting aerobatics as do ravens. Writing in 1924 the distinguished ornithologist Professor Kennedy Orton stated that "the raven is the most persistently and continuously persecuted bird in this country". He also stated that very few of the "Raven Crags" (Clog-y-fran) are used any more for rearing broods. It is true that the raven had been slowly and relentlessly driven from their old, established haunts.

Today there are very few ravens to be seen in these beloved Welsh uplands, the objects of wholesale slaughter on account of their admitted damage to the annual crop of young lambs and because of their large size – the largest all-black British bird – which has rendered them easily seen and shot.

---

8. It is now possible to descend directly down the long south-western flank for 2,750 feet to Nant Peris but if time allows it is best to continue on down to the great col between Y Garn and Glyder Fawr called Bwlch Blaen-Cwm-Idwal, "the pass at the head of Cwm Idwal". A stream drains from Llyn y Cwn, an almost square lakelet under Glyder Fawr's northern flank, and drops into the complicated volcanic scenery at the top of Twll Du, "the black hole" more popularly known as "The Devil's Kitchen", and finally plunges into that notorious chasm and so down to join the waters of Llyn Idwal far below.

9. And now we turn back to the south-west and across the ill-drained moorland that leads to steepening ground and Cwm Cneifio. There is a track now which winds down, never far from the tumbling Afon Lâs, into the steep fields above Gwastadnant. Once the road is gained at Gwastadnant, maybe a good hour or more from Twll Du, it is but a few minutes' walk down to the starting point at Nant Peris.

The Devil's Kitchen

Thomas Pennant ventured to "look down this dreadful aperture, and found its horrors far from being lessened" in 1780; C. F. Holland wrote in 1924 that the normal route up the Devil's Kitchen "must undoubtedly be regarded as the least safe of the greater Welsh climbs", though there may be even less stable routes on Snowdonian cliffs today. Seen from a low level in Cwm Idwal the expanse of cliff split down its centre by Twll Du exhibits very clearly the syncline of rock layers which is one of the numerous downfolds found in the rock stratum of Snowdonia. But from our chasm-top viewpoint we can look down into the rift, wet and dark and hung with ferns and numerous rare plants due to the high lime content of the volcanic tuffs here and the humidity caused by the almost continuous spray. Early June finds the very rare Snowdon lily (Lloydia serotina) which should on no account be plucked or gathered for this region is the only place in Britain where it is found. On this same cliff the Arctic saxifrage (*Saxifraga nivalis*) grows, noted here as early as 1805.

Chapter 17

TWENTY SNOWDONIAN SUMMITS

Route: Pen-y-Pass – Gallt-y-Wenallt – Lliwedd – Y Wyddfa -Crib Goch – Gwastadnant – Elidir Fawr – Myndd Perfedd – Glyder Fawr -Glyder Fach – Tryfan – Pen-yr-Oleu-wen – Yr Elen – Carnedd Llewelyn – Foel Fras – Carnedd Llewelyn – Tal-y-Braich – Capel Curig

Distance: 37 miles.

Grade: Extremely Strenuous

Starting Point: Pen-y-Pass (map refence: 647558)

Maps: Ordnance Survey "Landranger" (1:50,000) Sheet 115 (Snowdon and Surrounding Area); Ordnance Survey "Outdoor Leisure" (1:25,000) Sheet 17 (Snowdonia – Snowdon and Conwy Valley Areas).

There stands a cairn of rough stones in the heart of Cwm Glas Mawr, on a level of grassy tussocks above the broken cliffs that drop to the lower cwm. I built that cairn some summers ago to mark the site of a cache of food and drink to be used on a following day.

I left food and drink in five other places among the Snowdonian hills too. One upon the rushy slope of Gallt y Wenallt, one upon the summit rocks of Elidir Fawr and another above Bwlch Tryfan. The next lay sheltered below Pen yr Oleu wen's top and the last cairn-covered on Carnedd Llewelyn. These supplies were to help me walk over twenty summits in a day, to climb up and down approximately 30,000 feet for pleasure, to walk a new way among the hills, between sun and shadow.

Each morning dawned grey and the hills sat cloud-soaked. Each morning at half past three I looked out and returned to bed. On the last morning, at the usual time, I looked out to the black columns and the sky was blue – no clouds, but a rough, west wind.

It was half past four as I walked along the Miners' Track and crossed Cwm Dyli. A russet band lay across the Denbigh Moors and the wind was strong in gusts. Pale, flat light filled every rock cranny as I ate the first food beyond Gallt y Wenallt's top. On the uttermost rock splinter of Lliwedd's West Peak an hour later the sunshine reached me at last and upon the next summit of Y Wyddfa I came up from the lee side of the ridge and met a strong wind, roaring gustily up the slopes.

The author on the north ridge of Tryfan

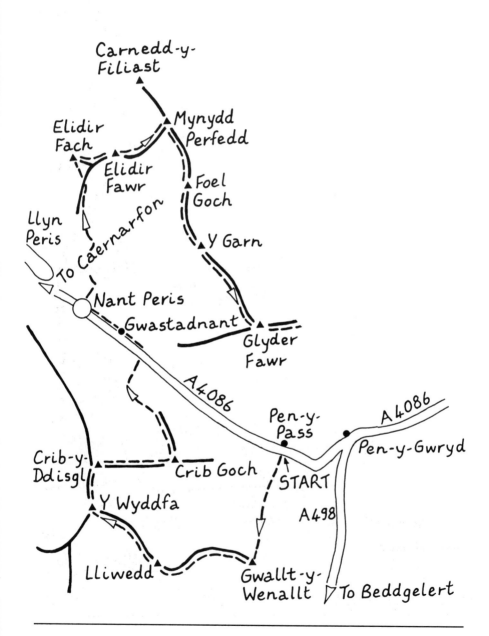

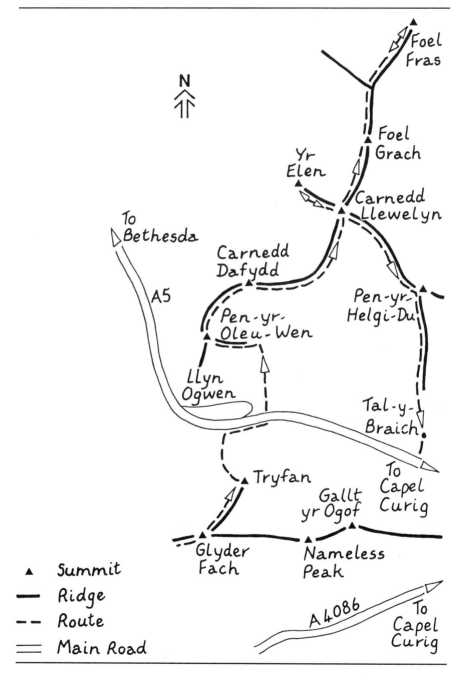

N

Foel Fras

Foel Grach

Yr Elen

Carnedd Llewelyn

To Bethesda

Carnedd Dafydd

A5

Pen-yr-Helgi-Du

Pen-yr-Oleu-Wen

Llyn Ogwen

Tal-y-Braich

Tryfan

To Capel Curig

Gallt yr Ogof

Glyder Fach

Nameless Peak

▲ Summit

— Ridge

-- Route

= Main Road

A4086

To Capel Curig

Raven wings tilted across the grey below the north-facing crest and on the descent along to Crib y Ddisgl I wondered if this was just an early morning blow or going to be a day-long gale. The latter proved to be the case, though the sun shone until evening.

The thousand feet drop from Crib Goch's summit into Cwm Glas by the north ridge took ten minutes and soon I was eating by that already-mentioned cairn as the Dinorwig Quarry siren echoed up from below.

A lovely sunny morning in June among the high hills. All about were innumerable alpines in full bloom and ground beetles were everywhere. It was a shame to go on. One hour later the steep, broken slopes falling to the Afon Nant Peris and Gwastadnant had been negotiated, the Titanian woods of oak and leaning hazel above Nant Peris had been trodden under and the cuckoo's call came across the even grass slopes of Elidir Fawr. The south-east face of this giant hill-mass is one of my favourites, long and almost unbroken and spacious to every vapour and often dotted with Welsh Mountain ewes and lambs. There can be no bigger mountain-side south of the Highlands, two thousand feet from base to summit ridge and catching all the morning's bright sunlight. I was thankful for the bottle of lemonade placed a few days before beneath a broken wall where rushes grew luxuriantly.

From the sweeping, shattered ridge Elidir Fach (2,964 feet) rolled away a quarter of a mile to the north and that was my next summit. The wind was very strong on the crossing from this lesser peak to its greater neighbour but by eleven o'clock the cache upon the 3,029 foot summit of Elidir Fawr was reached. It was later than I had anticipated when still in the valley, though even then it was my belief that by 2.30 p.m. I could be ascending the first slopes of the Carneddau.

Dark-shadowed clouds crowded low over the Carneddau summits and from this Elidir perch the very air seemed lonely. The strong wind blew, the clouds cast black gloom north-eastwards and I hadn't seen a soul that day. Now, however, it was time to climb on, down the terraces of the scree with wide views over into the northern cwm which contains Llyn Marchlyn Mawr. High up on the north-eastern slope of Elidir Fawr peers Craig Cwrwgl. This is the most isolated peak in Snowdonia, a great wedge of cliff that claims to possess a summit attainable only after many feet of rock climbing.

On over the grassy, sheep-dense top of Mynydd Perfedd and so by a rocky way to the lovely Foel Goch and giant Y Garn, the armchair mountain at the head of the Nant Ffrancon which cradles a favourite pool of earlier days, Llyn Clyd. I gained the top of Y Garn half an hour after noon, just eight hours after leaving Pen-y-Pass; with the sun still shining here I could look to the eastern mountains carrying wisps of grey mist around their heads.

Whilst approaching the summit of this mountain it had been my guess that I would arrive on Glyder Fawr at two o'clock. The descent to the top of the great syncline above Twll Du passed swiftly and the highest Glyder was crossed by 1.20 p.m. The summits of Glyder Fawr and Glyder Fach are separated by that well-known, mile-long shoulder and on this I met the first people of the day. In twenty minutes I had reached the lower top and with the sun still hot, the wind still strong and Glyder Fawr forming a blue-grey foreground to the great bulk of the Snowdon massif behind I prepared to descend the Bristly Ridge to the cache on Bwlch Tryfan. During earlier hours this drop of one thousand feet had built itself up as one to be anticipated with pleasure, an interesting change from the up-and-down of the hills behind.

In fact, the descent of this steep rock ridge took fifty minutes of swing-down and step-round before the col was crossed and then up the short, steep way to the 3,010 feet summit of Tryfan, triple crowned and a wondrous viewpoint from which to search the southern corners of the Carneddau; then down the famous two thousand feet of the west face to Telford's highroad to Holyhead. This steep fall from Tryfan-top to Llyn Ogwen can consume much time if the wrong line is taken, though good route-finding can bring one to the bottom in a short time. My route was by Y Gully (first ascended, it is thought, in 1894), then by the Brag Rocks and so on down. In thirty minutes I was walking along the road and at Glan Dena turned northwards towards the Carneddau. It was half-past three and the sun was still shining.

Upon the dry, sheep-shorn turf between tall boulders the way led up, not far to the west of the trickling Afon Lloer, the Stream of the Moon, draining lofty Ffynnon Lloer, Lakelet of the Moon, that dappled pool on the floor of Cwm Lloer, with red scree slopes rising all around; rising a thousand feet to the curtain of the mountain wall linking Carnedd Dafydd with Pen yr Oleu wen. Ffynnon Lloer lake holds 3-4 ounce trout but is rarely fished.

Once the little lake was on my level I turned to the left and up the steep, shelving east ridge of Pen yr Oleu-wen. This ascent was out of the bumpety wind and as the sun went round there were sections hundreds of feet high when I climbed in shade; shade which made Craig Lloer dark and featureless. The 2,200 feet rise from Glan Dena to the top of Pen yr Oleu-wen took nearly two hours but the clouds on the Carneddau had dispersed and the sun shone over the hills I had traversed earlier.

The lovely dip-and-rise from this summit to Carnedd Dafydd invited a change of pace and I ran over the scree and wind-torn turf, past the two pre-historic burial mounds and over Dafydd's top (fourth highest summit of Snowdonia) at six p.m. I ran on, on and over and up the south face of Carnedd Llewelyn to a height of 3,200 feet. At this altitude my route turned north-westwards, along this contour to the wild col between Carnedd Llewelyn and Yr Elen, outlier *par excellence*. Up the slaty side I went, with a clear view downwards to lonely Ffynnon Caseg, 550 feet beneath. A single sheep browsed on the level summit platform, turning away as I came up.

Just below, it seemed, and almost touchable, was the confluence of the Afon Caseg with the Afon Llafar and, just beyond, the smoke and shadows and slate of Bethesda; this side of the lowering sun.

My rucksack was en-cairned on the 3,484 foot top of Carnedd Llewelyn and this was reached by 7.30 p.m. I left it there to be collected on my return from the crossing of the three last hills of the day.

Fifteen hours and seventeen peaks had passed and the sun was going yellow in the haze over Anglesey. Northwards now, over Foel Grach and over the slight curves of the last-but-one summit I strode. Yr Aryg (the Long Ridge) is barely discernible, a mere swelling of the broad mountain backbone where it forks on to the burial-mounded top of Drosgl in the north-west and to the far hill of Drum and Tal-y-Fan in the north-east.

Fading light, the moaning wind and the featureless angles of the
northern Carneddau. The distant brown line turned into a weather-
beaten wall on the top of the last and farthest hill, Foel Fras, along the
north-eastern arm towards Drum and Tal-y-Fan.

Anglesey and Menai Straits, from the summit of Foel Fras (3,091 ft)

I reached the top at 8.10 p.m. and was surprised at the apparent
proximity of the north coast, of Aber, Bangor and Beaumaris, of Penmon
Point, the Dutchman Bank and the tump of Puffin Island beyond, a
grey-black whale-back set in the golden sea.

Fifteen and a half hours after leaving Pen-y-Pass and fourteen hours and
forty minutes after breasting the first summit I set off on the long dusky
return. The wind still blew across those grassy ridges. Soon I was
running down over the narrow ridge above Craig yr Ysfa and along the
loose traverse at 2,300 feet on Pen yr Helgi-du's western flank. The light
had almost gone, the wind had dropped, the sky was clear and the first
stars were winking. The only sounds were the Afon Llugwy below and a
disturbed ewe somewhere to the east. The full moon rose like a great

orange over the Denbigh moors as I got down to Tal-y-Braich farm. In a few minutes I would reach the Holyhead road and start the long walk back to Pen-y-Pass by way of Capel Curig. But the farmer at Tal-y-Braich must have the last word. As I left the yard he said: "Such a lovely day it's been, and such a warm evening; just right for a walk now."

THE ROUTE

A brief itinerary of the route described in the foregoing walk is set out below for those who would like to follow it. Times are given to provide a rough guide to planning.

Peak	Height	Time
(Pen-y-Pass)	1,169 ft.	4.35 a.m.
Gallt y Wenallt	2,032 ft.	5.25 a.m.
Lliwedd West Peak	2,947 ft.	6.25 a.m.
Y Wyddfa	3,560 ft.	7.05 a.m.
Crib y Ddisgl	3,493 ft.	7.20 a.m.
Crib Goch	3,023 ft.	7.50 a.m.
(Cache Two-Cwm Glas Mawr)	2,100 ft.	8.00 a.m.
(Gwastadnant)	390 ft.	9.00 a.m.
Elidir Fach	2,964 ft.	10.50 a.m.
Elidir Fawr	3,029 ft.	11.00 a.m.
Mynydd Perfedd	2,664 ft.	11.40 a.m.
Foel Goch	2,726 ft.	12.00 noon
Y Garn	3,104 ft.	12.30 p.m.
Glyder Fawr	3,279 ft	1.20 p.m.
Glyder Fach	3,262 ft	1.40 p.m.
Tryfan	3,010 ft	3.00 p.m.
(Holyhead Road)	984 ft.	3.25 p.m.
Pen yr Oleu-wen	3,210 ft.	5.20 p.m.
Carnedd Dafydd	3,426 ft.	6.10 p.m.
Yr Elen	3,151 ft.	7.00 p.m.
Carnedd Llewelyn	3,484 ft.	7.25 p.m.
Foel Grach	3,195 ft.	7.45 p.m.
Yr Aryg	2,950 ft.	7.55 p.m.
Foel Fras	3,091 ft.	8.10 p.m.
(Tal-y-Braich Farm)	1,000 ft.	10.15 p.m.

Chapter 18

NEWBOROUGH WARREN AND LLANDDWYN ISLAND

Route: Newborough – Newborough Warren – Llanddwyn Bay – Llanddwyn Island – Cerrigmawr – Newborough

Distance: 7.5 miles.

Grade: Moderate

Starting Point: Newborough village (map reference: 424657)

Maps: Ordnance Survey "Landranger" (1:50,000) Sheet 114 (Anglesey); Ordnance Survey "Pathfinder" (1:25,000) Sheet 768

The south-western angle of Anglesey is occupied by a great area of sand dunes, an area bounded by the tidal sands of Malltraeth, and the narrow, western mouth of the Menai Straits. In few places does the land of Newborough Warren reach over one hundred feet. Rabbits ran everywhere, burrowing easily among the dunes and the name "Warren" was most appropriate. Today, however, much of the area is devoted to coniferous plantation and the rabbits have been excluded from much of this Forestry Commission land. The conifers have done well here and their roots help to anchor the loose sands. The acres of pines against a background of yellow dunes and blue sea are very reminiscent of Les Landes in western France. Much of Newborough Warren is now a National Nature Reserve under the care of the Countryside Council for Wales.

Llanddwyn Island

Saint Dwynwen died here on January 25th in A.D. 465, a holy man who came here to this lonely isle to seek peace by the unchanging sea. The name of the island is seen to come from this man's own name. A cross was erected here in 1879 by the owner of the island, F. G. Wynn, in a commanding position.

At the centre of the island are the ruins of an ancient church, a neglected and sea-blasted structure now almost forgotten. For many centuries Llanddwyn was obviously a holy place, beginning with Saint Dwynwen and continuing with the now-ruined church. Nearby is another Celtic cross of relatively recent origin. Upon it is the inscription:

They lie around, did living tread
This living ground – now silent – dead.

- presumably marking this ancient burial ground originally attached to the church.

Because the island stands out from the general line of Anglesey's coast the place was always a hazard to shipping. Upon the southern tip are the remains of a tower which once served as a look-out and on which could be placed a fire to mark the place for ships at sea. For sixty-seven years (between 1840 and 1907) there was a lifeboat station here, too.

At the western extremity of the island is the white-painted lighthouse which was once much taller and manned by the keepers who lived in the cottages nearby. In more recent times it was chopped short to 30 feet and today is an unmanned lighthouse exhibiting its 900 candela-power light every 2.5 seconds fifty feet above sea level.

The scatter of rocks lying off the island is a good place to watch for Atlantic grey seals on still days and on the short cliffs dropping to the sea many birds nest, including the common gull and kittiwake. Common terns skim in characteristic light and buoyant flight over the rocks draped with sea campion, the white blooms of early summer contrasting with the pink flowers of thrift on every sunny corner above the tide. Lying here and listening one is able to pick out the "kik-kik-kik" of the common terns and the soft "tchu-ick" of roseate terns above the lapping of water upon seaweed and rocks below. Away to the south, over the waters of Caernarfon Bay, the great pyramids of the Rivals rise straight out of the sea and lead the eye on towards westernmost Lleyn.

The Route

1. From the village of Newborough take the lane westwards which curves down into the sandhills, a relatively new forest-road. After almost two interesting, wooded miles the car park area near the sea is gained and over a line of dunes we look out into Llanddwyn Bay with its long sweep of beach curving round towards the west to Llanddwyn Island. Making for this low and rock-girt isle the isthmus at Gwddw Llanddwyn is soon reached (map reference: 391635). It is easy to imagine what things were like here a few centuries ago, the island then truly isolated from Anglesey by shallow water as far inland, perhaps, as the fifty-foot contour below Cerrigmawr (map reference: 393638). Slowly the channel filled with blown and drifted sand and today Llanddwyn is rarely isolated completely.

2. Walking now along the island we enter a different world, a world more

Hebridean than Welsh, an isle with true oceanic feeling attributable, no doubt, to the way in which it sticks well out into the Irish Sea. A whole holiday might be spent here with camera and sketch-pad, for there are remains of human activity to contrast with the natural life of sea and shore and grassy island-top.

3. Turning back to the north-west we walk along the narrow isthmus, and if on foot from Newborough, make straight inland along the footpath which skirts Cerrig-mawr and Bryn-llwyd, rocky hills or knolls reaching one hundred feet above sea level. The forestry plantations which have developed here since World War Two have converted this open dune-land to enclosed coniferous woodland with no vistas over land or sea. Llanddwyn to Newborough is about three miles.

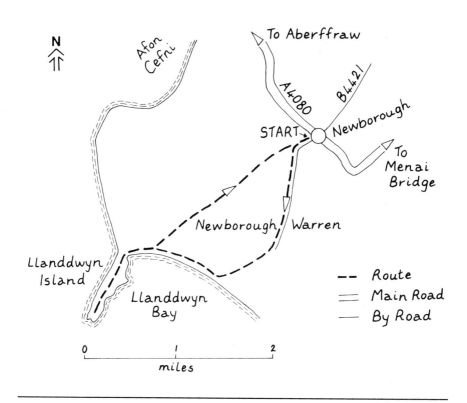

Chapter 19

CARMEL HEAD AND CLOUD SHADOWS ON THE SEA

Route: Llanrhyddlad – Church Bay – Ynys-y-fydlyn – Carmel Head – Mynachdy Farm –
Llanfairynghornwy – Llanrhyddlad or Church Bay

Distance: 8.5 miles.

Grade: Moderate

Starting Point: Church Bay (map reference: 300892)

Maps: Ordnance Survey "Landranger" (1:50,000) Sheet 114 (Anglesey); Ordnance
Survey "Pathfinder" (1:25,000) Sheet 733

Would it be for the best to live in a place of great and happy memory?
Maybe it is that we think such dreams would be wonderful but, after all,
such places are best left in the mind as retreats to escape to for long,
nostalgic glimpses. Familiarity perhaps does breed contempt or, at least,
lack of respect – a taking-for-granted and casualness which partially
destroys the golden memories.

I have often thought a remote corner of north-western Anglesey would
be a delight to live in but would not the spice and the gilded frame into
which I have placed it in memory be somewhat eroded by day-to-day
contact? Perhaps it is better to live in a sooty back-street and imagine
how wonderful it would be to reside in an Elizabethan manor-house.
Living there would make the back-street seem not so bad after all. And
so it is that north-western Anglesey is a promised dreamland of jewelled
memories, let it remain so.

This part of the island is well scattered with tiny villages with a common
prefix – Llanynghenedl, Llanfachraeth, Llanddeusant (the old windmill
here – map reference: 341852 – is the last of its kind in Anglesey),
Llanfaethlu, Llanrhyddlad, Llanfechell and Llanfairynghornwy.

The Route

1. A long, sea-side walk can be had by taking the lane from Llanrhyddlad down to the relatively quiet shore of Church Bay and then making northwards by Porth Swtan and so, in two miles, to the rock-edged bay called Porthybri-bys. Another small headland is crossed and there below is a shallow valley with a pool lying back behind the high water mark and edged with flag irises. Herons wade gently here and hares chase across the open pastures behind. A shorter walk to this shallow valley can be taken if one leaves the lane near Taldrwst (map reference: 309919) and descends directly to the west, reaching the coast in a little over one mile.

Ynys-y-Fydlyn

The finest feature of this valley-mouth by the sea is the little isle of Ynys-y-fydlyn lying immediately off-shore and accessible at low tide without even getting one's feet wet. Here we have often lain among the short-cropped grass and the flowering thrift, looking out over the blue-and-white sea to the hazy rocks of the Skerries under a summer sky. Sea birds wheel overhead and call with little rest, an oyster catcher "bleeping" as it passes close by in characteristic direct, business-like flight. Just behind the islet is a complex of small but interesting sea-caves where one can wander when the tide is out.

2. Going northwards we approach the last bulge of the west coast before the very "corner" of Anglesey. On these little cliffs many gulls nest and one is subjected to continual attack if walking here in the nesting season. I have come across the rough and twiggy nest of a chough here, too, the all-black bird flying to-and-fro' overhead, its curved red bill and red legs visible in the May sunshine. And then we are looking into the tiny, rocky bay or inlet of Porth-y-dyfn, and not far beyond is the final thrust of old, hard rock which forms Carmel Head – or Trwyn-y-Gader to be more correct – and here we can look down into the narrow rifts of lapping sea and pick out many species of seaweeds, of shell creatures and the occasional inquisitive Atlantic grey seal bobbing its head up like a swimming spaniel.

3. The way back follows the northern coast for half a mile or so then makes southwards for a narrow track leading to Mynachdy Farm and so to the lane winding by the scattered habitations of Llanfairynghornwy; how the name rolls off the tongue, a truly Welsh sound. By looking at

the map it is not a difficult matter to pick out a route back to either
Llanrhyddlad village with its church with a fine spire (map reference:
332891), or down to Church Bay.

The great charm of a walk such as this often lies in the opportunities that
arise for listening and long looks, at the quiet charms of the coast and
the serenity of the sea.

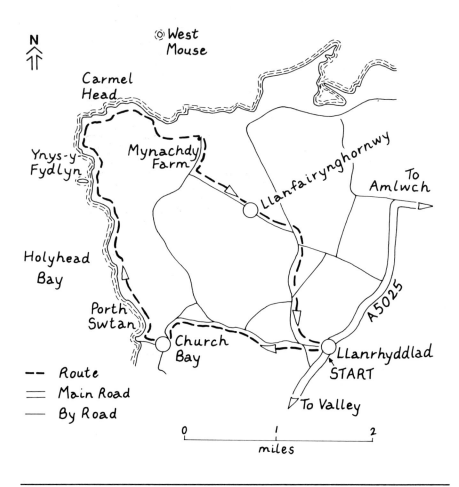

Magic by the Sea

Lying on my back among the summer grasses on some Anglesey headland a lark sings behind, over inland pastures edged with the gold of gorse. High above in the blue firmament white cloud-islets drift into and out of sight, small vessels with sails set to catch any passing breeze in these lazy hours. A drone in the wild vetches close by indicates that something, somewhere is busy in the sunlight from far away. A haze of bluebells and hedges with red campion and ragged robin drift to and fro'; a sugar-prince rides the sky on sunbeams cast far and wide over the lines of blue-green sea. The blue haze of bluebells merges into an outline of distant hills, likewise blue and soft; like velvet on hazy mid-summer dawns. Hills of other days, maybe, where youth is retained and youth recalled; crag-days and ridge-days under a sparkling sky when the smoke from the mountain train rose directly upwards for hundreds of feet and the sunlight burned along the crest of Crib Goch and turned our limbs to mahogany. Then the lap of a little wave on the lichened rocks below and the voice of a meadow-pipit bring me back to my place near the sea and full consciousness.

INDEX

Notes

Notes

Notes

Notes

Explore the countryside with Sigma!. We have a wide selection of guides to individual towns, plus outdoor activities centred on walking and cycling in the great outdoors throughout England and Wales.
Here are some recent highlights:

PEAK DISTRICT DIARY - Roger Redfern
An evocative book, celebrating the glorious countryside of the Peak District. The book is based on Roger's popular column in *The Guardian* newspaper and is profusely illustrated with stunning photographs. *£6.95*

I REMAIN, YOUR SON JACK - J. C. Morten (edited by Sheila Morten)
A collection of almost 200 letters, as featured on BBC TV, telling the moving story of a young soldier in the First World War. Profusely illustrated with contemporary photographs. *£8.95*

There are many books for outdoor people in our catalogue, including:

HERITAGE WALKS IN THE PEAK DISTRICT
- Clive Price

EAST CHESHIRE WALKS
- Graham Beech

WEST CHESHIRE WALKS
- Jen Darling

WEST PENNINE WALKS
- Mike Cresswell

NEWARK AND SHERWOOD RAMBLES
- Malcolm McKenzie

RAMBLES AROUND MANCHESTER
- Mike Cresswell

WESTERN LAKELAND RAMBLES
- Gordon Brown

WELSH WALKS: Dolgellau and the Cambrian Coast
- Laurence Main and Morag Perrott

WELSH WALKS: Aberystwyth and District
- Laurence Main and Morag Perrott

CYCLING IN THE COTSWOLDS
– Stephen Hill

OFF-BEAT CYCLING IN THE PEAK DISTRICT
- Clive Smith

MORE OFF-BEAT CYCLING IN THE PEAK DISTRICT
- Clive Smith

50 BEST CYCLE RIDES IN CHESHIRE
- edited by Graham Beech

- all of these walking and cycling books are currently £6.95 each.

For long-distance walks enthusiasts, we have several books including:

THE GREATER MANCHESTER BOUNDARY WALK
- Graham Phythian

THE THIRLMERE WAY
- Tim Cappelli

THE MARCHES WAY
- Les Lumsdon

- all £6.95 each

We also publish:

A guide to the 'Pubs of Old Lancashire'

A fabulous series of 'Pub Walks' books for many locations in the UK, all featuring access by public transport

A new series of investigations into the Supernatural, Myth and Magic

Superb illustrated books on Manchester's football teams

- plus many more entertaing and educational books being regularly added to our list.

All of our books are available from your local bookshop. In case of difficulty, or to obtain our complete catalogue, please contact:

Sigma Leisure,

1 South Oak Lane,

Wilmslow, Cheshire SK9 6AR

Phone: 0625 - 531035 Fax: 0625 - 536800

ACCESS and VISA orders welcome - call our friendly sales staff or use our 24 hour Answerphone service! Most orders are despatched on the day we receive your order - you could be enjoying our books in just a couple of days.

AUTHORS: if you have an interesting idea for a book, contact us for a rapid and expert decision. Note that we are not a 'Vanity Press' - all of our books earn royalties for their writers.